HOLY PLACES

HOLY PLACES

Barbara Calamari & Sandra DiPasqua

Viking Studio

VIKING STUDIO
Published by the Penguin Group
Penguin Putnum Inc., 375 Hudson Street,
New York, New York 10014, U.S.A.
Penguin Books Ltd, 80 Strand,
London WC2R 0RL, England
Penguin Books Australia Ltd, 250 Camberwell Road, Camberwell,
Victoria 3124, Australia
Penguin Books Canada Ltd, 10 Alcorn Avenue,
Toronto, Ontario, Canada M4V 3B2
Penguin Books India (P) Ltd, 11 Community Centre, Panchsheel Park
New Delhi - 110 017, India
Penguin Books (N.Z.) Ltd, Cnr Rosedale and Airborne Roads, Albany,
Auckland, New Zealand
Penguin Books (South Africa) (Pty) Ltd, 24 Sturdee Avenue,
Rosebank, Johanneburg 2196, South Africa

Penguin Books Ltd, Registered Offices:
Harmondsworth, Middlesex, England

First published in 2002 by Viking Studio.
a member of Penguin Putnam Inc.

1 3 5 7 9 10 8 6 4 2

CIP data available

ISBN 0-670-03081-3

This book is printed on acid-free paper. ∞

Printed in China
Set in Adobe Garamond
Designed by Sandra DiPasqua

Acknowledgments

We have many people to thank for the help we were given on this book. Our agent, Jim Fitzgerald from the Carol Mann Agency, came up with the idea for this project. Christopher Sweet and Michelle Li at Viking Studio for all their support. Karen Dottling did much of the initial gathering of research materials and Helen Quinn did some of our field work.

We are very grateful to Ted Feder and Linda Lee of Art Resources for helping us to arrange for the majority of our images. The New York Public Library has also been an invaluable source for pictures. In a book such as this, there are many obscure and hard to find pictures needed and we were very lucky to have the kind assistance of Ruth Moran at the Irish Tourist Board, Esther Gomez at the Spanish Tourist Board and Marina Ochoa, archivist for the Archdiocese of New Mexico. Each of them sent us sets of photographs, which did a great deal to improve our book. In addition we are extremely grateful to Suzanne da Rosa of Dos Mujeres Mexican Folk Art, www.mexican-folkart.com, and Georgia Alexandra Dering for supplying the visuals from Mexico City.

We'd also like to thank Louis and Paolo Turchioe for their maps, Debbie Rust for her much needed technical assistance, Carol Day and Pat Bates for their all around support of this project.

This book is dedicated to Louie Turchioe and Patricia A. Bates

Contents

Introduction

Sacred sites are as old as mankind. All civilizations recognize certain locations that are deemed to be special or divinely charged with energy. In some cases, religions rise and fall, but the holy site remains the same. In this book, *Holy Places,* we are detailing several of the most well-known and popular Catholic shrines. These locales attract as many of the faithful today as they did one thousand years ago. What we have attempted to do in this book is to research the original reasons why a place came to be known as a site of miraculous occurrences that would make pilgrims want to gather there. All of these places are dedicated to a certain saint or came about because of a miraculous incident. Many have strong groups of devotees. Instead of formal pilgrimages, most of the modern visits are conducted in group tours. At first glance, the crowds and the commercialism seem to deprive a place of its mystery. What we have found is that most of these places were considered holy in pre-Christian times and that present-day commercial traffic has not robbed them of their spiritual eminence. There is still something very powerful in the feeling a group that gathers there generates.

A place like Assisi literally emanates peace. Many say it is the shade of the pink stone that regulates the pulse into a less agitated state; others say the prayers of the millions of pilgrims descending on such a small place have to have some vibrational effect. When one walks into Chartres Cathedral, the fact is there is no way that such a building would have been constructed to serve commerce or industry. Because it was for spiritual purposes the very best was brought out in perfecting new techniques in glass, architecture and sculpture.

Most Catholics know the traditional stories of these sacred spots, but not many realize the effect these places held for pre-Christian cultures. The Virgin Mary had been seen in the regions surrounding Lourdes for hundreds of years before the healing waters of its grotto were revealed. Many saw Mary as a little three-foot woman, a traditional character in Celtic legend. To the indigenous people of that region she was always considered a member of the family, much like the Mexicans of today view Our Lady of Guadalupe. The Way of Saint James, known as El Camino Santiago, was most likely first mapped out by the ancient Celts. They developed a walking path guided by the stars and energy points in the earth known as ley lines. Likewise, the Druids worshiped a virgin mother at Chartres one hundred years before the birth of Christ.

We are not scholars and our research materials ranged from traditional Catholic texts, to various Web sites to travel, architectural, history and art books, including *Encyclopedia of Sacred Places* by Norbert C. Brockman. We also drew on firsthand experiences. In selecting these sites we tried to bring a variety of locations and sacred atmospheres into focus both in the visual and the literary sense. We have included immense basilicas like St. Peter's, a modest mission church in New Mexico and a holy mountain in Ireland. Each is equally important to Catholics, and a majority is important to people of all faiths. There are many sites we did not include in this selection due to length and time restrictions and what we have written here is by no means the final word on these holy places.

In our visual depictions we have also tried to show a variety of the innovations, art forms and portraits of these holy places and those who inspired them. We hope our readers will look at these places with fresh eyes and pay some of them a visit.

Assisi

11

Italy

Assisi

1

Italy

Left page: The frescoes lining the interior of the Basilica of Saint Francis brought immense changes in the course of art history and the basilica is considered the cradle of Italian painting.
Center: Saint Francis was known for his great love of all living things.
Right, bottom: The basilica and its attached monastery are made of the same pink stone as the town of Assisi.

Home to one of the greatest saints in all of Catholicism, Assisi is a revered site not only for Christians but also for Buddhists, Muslims and animists as well. Located in the geographical center of Italy, Umbria, its province is known as the green heart of Italy. Assisi overlooks the largest and most plentiful valley in an otherwise hilly terrain. Rich in vegetation, water, agriculture and wildlife, Assisi lives in complete harmony with Mount Subasio. Recognized as a blessed location long before Christianity, Assisi was founded by the Umbri tribe 865 years before the founding of Rome. The ancient town of Assisium came into existence around a holy spring that was later venerated by the Etruscans. Already settled in the pre-Roman era, Assisi still has extensive city walls dating to the second century B.C. When the Romans supplanted the Etruscans, they built a temple to the goddess Minerva around the holy spring. That temple, dating from 25 B.C., still stands in the town square, perfectly preserved. Minerva is the goddess of the arts, handicrafts and the professions; the Greeks identified her with the goddess Athena. Today the temple has been con-

·S·RVFI·   ·S·VICTO·

·S·FRAN CISCVS·   ·SCA·CLA RA·

Italy

verted into a Catholic church and the spring has dried up, but the sentiments of the ancient goddess permeate the town. Poetry, art and philosophy were revolutionized here, forever changing Western civilization.

The peaceful and mystical atmosphere of Assisi is little disturbed by the 4 to 5 million visitors it receives each year. Much of the town was built in the twelfth to fourteenth centuries from the pink stone found in Mount Subasio. It is thought that the stone itself has absorbed the prayers of so many pilgrims, stimulating peaceful feelings in the human heart. Because the town was only ninety miles north of Rome, it became one of the pontifical states ruled by the pope and, therefore, did not build up much industry as did neighboring regions of Italy. Though keeping it economically backward, this served to preserve the great natural beauty of its plant and animal life. Many attribute

The Temple of Minerva, dating from 25 B.C., stands perfectly preserved in the middle of Assisi.

this to the protection of its great native son, Saint Francis, who was born in A.D. 1181 or 1182.

Few saints have been able to communicate so relevantly through the ages to so many as Saint Francis of Assisi. Though he died in A.D. 1226, his message of nonmaterialism and simplicity and his love of all life both great and small inspire many of every faith. In his day, Francis taught by example, as Christ did. His plan was simple: to live as much like Christ and his disciples as possible. By living this way, he quietly but effectively challenged the decadence of the papacy and the Church government. The son of a wealthy cloth merchant, he was a fun-loving and pleasure-seeking young man who was greatly changed after being taken prisoner in a local war with Perugia. In the neglected church of San Damiano, he heard the crucifix speak to him: "Go and repair my house, which you see is falling down." He took these instructions literally, embarrassing and enraging his father. Ultimately, he renounced his inheritance, throwing his clothing in the street. The bishop of Assisi provided Francis with his new garments, the brown robes of a monk. Eventually, he was joined by a few other young men of his social stature, and in 1209 he wrote his first holy rule. He embraced poverty and was intent on living as the original apostles of Christ did, traveling, preaching and begging for alms. In an Italy torn by fighting between towns and families, Francis promoted peace. At a time when the Church was sponsoring the bloody Crusades, Francis was preaching understanding. He called all animals brother and sister and exhorted every creature to honor its Creator. His order of mendicant friars, known as the Franciscans, earned him a huge following throughout Europe. Even in his own lifetime, pilgrims came to hear him preach or receive his blessing. Without using force or any confrontational methods they did much to change and inspire the thinking of the young people of their day.

Saint Clare was the beautiful daughter of an Assisi nobleman who had turned down several offers of marriage. After she heard Saint Francis speak when she was eighteen years old, she made up her mind to leave her life of privilege and follow him. At that time, homes in Assisi had two doors—one for regular use and the door of the dead, used only for funerals. Clare left home through the door of the dead, renouncing the material world. Met in secret by Francis and his friars, her long hair was cut off and in 1215 she founded the Poor Clares. This was an order of women, with a rule written by Saint Francis himself, owning no property and existing solely on alms. Because of Francis's living example, Clare became one of the foremost religious contemplatives of her time. Her order of nuns is still in existence, in places all over the world. She is buried in the Basilica of St. Clare and is considered one of the great souls of Assisi.

Francis was a mystic who directly communed with Christ and Mary through his visions. He welcomed the opportunity to communicate with all

Next page: The lower church. The basilica is composed of three sanctuaries, one over another. The arts were very important to Saint Francis and his basilica is covered from top to bottom with paintings and frescoes.

people regardless of their social background and invented the creche, or manger scene, to illustrate the miracle of the Nativity for the poor who flocked to his little church. He was also a great poet, composing the first poems in the Italian language, making them accessible to the average person who did not have an educated background. His "Canticle of the Sun" and "Canticle of Creatures," inspired by his life with nature in the Mount Subasio region, are considered among the finest poems in Italian literature. The "Fioretti," or "Little Flowers of Saint Francis," are much loved and widely read to this day. A compilation of stories from the thirteenth century, they detail the life of the friars and their joy and enthusiasm for their work. In 1224, while praying alone on the secluded mountain of La Verna, Francis became the first saint to know the suffering of the crucified Christ by receiving the stigmata (spontaneously appearing wounds on the hands, feet and side, corresponding to the torments of Christ on the cross). These wounds stayed with him for the remaining two years of his life, causing him much suffering, which he bore with serenity. Francis died in 1226 and was declared a saint two years later in 1228. This was the same year that the cornerstone of the Basilica of St. Francis was laid in Assisi.

Built between A.D. 1228 and 1253, the Basilica of St. Francis is considered one of Italy's most important monuments. The short period of construction, rare for a church of this tremendous size, is often explained as a measure of the great love the people of the time had for Saint Francis. The church is composed of three sanctuaries, one over another, and is one of the earliest specimens of Gothic architecture in Italy. The body of Saint Francis was hidden in the church in 1230 by his order of friars. Because of the great demand for saints' relics, and fear of theft,

*Right page:
Giotto
fresco of
Saint Francis's
receiving
the stigmata.*

the true resting place of the body was kept a secret until its discovery in 1810. His tomb was finally opened to the public in 1818. It is impossible to overestimate the importance of the Basilica of St. Francis to art history. It is frescoed from top to bottom by the leading artists of the day: Cimabue, Giotto and Simone Martini. Because Saint Francis's life so mirrored that of Jesus Christ, it was allowed to be depicted in a series of twenty-eight scenes by the artist Giotto. This was the first time in hundreds of years that painters were free to create scenes of nature and diverse groups of humanity without being limited by the strictures of abstract and idealized consecrated themes. Never before had everyday life been depicted in paintings. Instead of seeing a stagnant portrait, the illiterate were able to read the story of Saint Francis through these paintings and understand his message of God's love for all creatures. Faith became visualized and all artists were inspired to work in a totally different way. For this reason, the basilica is considered the cradle of Italian painting.

To this day, Assisi receives a steady stream of pilgrims of different faiths from all over the world. Most come to visit the basilicas of Francis and Clare, the hermitage in the mountains and the Portiuncula, which is contained inside the Basilica of Our Lady of the Angels. This church, built in the mid-1500s and modeled on St. Peter's Basilica in Rome, lies three quarters of a mile outside the town of Assisi. It is an important site for Franciscan pilgrims because it was constructed around the Portiuncula ("a little portion"), the chapel where Saint Francis recognized his vocation and the cell he died in. This was his most permanent home after the Benedictines presented it to him in 1211. The little chapel was originally erected in A.D. 353 by hermits from the Valley of

Detail of the basilica. The short time it took to construct such an immense building was considered a testament of the love the people of Assisi had for Francis.

Josaphat who had brought relics from the grave of the Blessed Virgin. The chapel passed into the possession of Saint Benedict in A.D. 516. The name Our Lady of the Angels is said to be attributed to the singing of angels that had frequently been heard there. The original buildings housing the first Franciscans were gradually replaced in order to accommodate the ever-increasing number of visiting pilgrims.

Throughout history, Umbria and Assisi have always exuded a sacred atmosphere. Saint Francis strongly characterized these spiritual feelings with his deep love of Christ and the Catholic faith. Through his inspiration, human achievements have reached divine levels. When he prayed, the bright light in his raptures caused him to cry, but he could not bear to stop. His followers, worried that he would ruin his eyesight, attempted to intervene but he replied, "We are the same as flies, attracted to light." It is the essence of this light that millions of pilgrims still flock to Assisi to experience.

Italy

The Catacombs

Rome

2

The Catacombs

On May 31, 1578, while laborers were working in a vineyard near the Via Salaria, one of the oldest roads in Rome, the ground collapsed, exposing an ancient underground room. Decorated with frescoes and inscriptions in Greek and Latin, it led to a tunnel of what appeared to be an amazing subterranean city. Forgotten and perfectly preserved for more than one thousand years, this extensive complex of underground tombs, chapels and small meeting rooms was actually the resting place of millions of early Christians dating back to the first century A.D. No other place offers such a glimpse into the very source of the spirituality of those first practitioners of the religion that shook the Roman Empire to its core and eventually revolutionized the world.

The word "catacomb" is derived from the Latin *ad catacumbas,* meaning "at the hollows," a phrase that referred to the burial chambers at a hollow south of Rome. Human burial in subterranean rock chambers was an ancient

Left page: Three tomb chambers in the catacomb of San Sebastian give the illusion of an underground city street. Center: Statue of Saint Sebastian by Bernini. Right, bottom: Basilica of San Sebastian on the Via Appia was originally built in the fourth century over the entrance of the catacombs where saints Peter and Paul had been temporarily interred.

pre-Christian, pre-Roman custom in the Mediterranean. The earth is composed of tufa, or soft stone, and is very easy to excavate. According to Roman law, inherited from the Etruscans, all burials had to take place outside the sacred ground of the city itself. In 312 B.C. the Appia Antica, a four-lane highway eventually stretching to Brindisi, was constructed and paved. In ancient times it provided Rome with its chief route for conquering the East, enabling it to become one of the greatest empires in human history. Today the Appia Antica is best known for the tombs and catacombs that line it. Two thousand years ago, it was one of the most prominent roads leading to the city, thus it became a popular place for cemeteries and the mausoleums of the wealthy.

Eventually, the more established citizens of Rome preferred cremation. By the first century A.D., only Christians, Jews and a minority of the pagan population chose underground burial. Christians rejected the custom of cremation; they preferred burial, just as Christ was buried, because they felt they had to respect the bodies that would one day rise from the dead. Since much of the Christian population was poor people who did not own family burial plots, many of the first-century Christians were interred in common open-air cemeteries where pagans were also buried. Saint Peter himself was buried in the great public "necropolis" ("city of the dead") on Vatican Hill, open to anyone. By the second half of the second century, wealthy Romans newly converted to Christianity opened up their burial grounds to those of the faith. The problem of space limitation was solved by digging underground burial chambers. In its simplest form, a catacomb consisted of several underground galleries and rooms in a rectangular or grid pattern. Recesses, known as loculi, were cut into the walls, one above the other, to receive the bodies of one to four family members. Persons of distinction were buried in stone coffins or carved sarcophagi placed in arched niches. The tombs of martyrs, usually in separate chambers, served as altars. As Christianity gained converts and burials

Left page: Third-century Christian fresco of the Madonna and Child. While art on the pagan tombs portrayed loss and sorrow, the Christians tried to depict scenes of everlasting life. Center: Tomb of Clodius Hermes in the catacomb of San Sebastian. The wealthy had elaborate rooms of tombs while the majority of those buried here were placed in large dormitories or galleries.

First-floor gallery of the catacomb of Priscilla. Early Christians referred to their burial grounds as "sleeping places" resembling vast dormitories with row upon row of resting places.

Rome

Crypt of San Sebastian. The catacombs had rooms where the ancient Christians met and celebrated their funeral rites.

Rome

multiplied, the catacombs were expanded into honeycombs of galleries. These excavations were the responsibilty of a specialized guild of workers called fossores ("grave diggers"). Their way was lit by openings cut in the vault of a crypt or along the galleries called lucemaria ("skylights") or by the faint light of lamps. Baskets and bags were used to carry the dirt away. The lucemaria then remained open, providing light and air for visitors. As one level was filled, staircases were dug and a second, third, fourth or even fifth level of galleries was excavated below.

The burials of the early Christians were extremely spare and simple. The corpses, in imitation of Christ, were wrapped in a sheet or

Catacomb of San Sebastian. This interior of a tomb shows elaborate mosaic and fresco work.

shroud and placed in the loculi without any kind of coffin. The loculi were sealed with a slab of marble or by tiles fixed with mortar. On the tombstone the name of the deceased was sometimes engraved, along with a Christian symbol or invocation to find peace in heaven. Oil lamps and small vases containing perfumes were placed beside the tomb.

The early Christians of Rome lived in a society that treated them with hostility and suspicion. When it was first brought to Rome, after the crucifixion of Christ, Roman authorities were indifferent to this new faith. Christians attracted many converts because of their belief in life after death and in brotherly love and the charitable

way they lived their lives. Christianity became particularly attractive to the poor and servant class, giving them hope for a better life in the next world. The Roman authorities began to recognize the Christians as a threat to the power of the state. The Christians, while remaining good citizens, refused to sacrifice to the ancient pagan gods or worship the emperor. Senate decrees from A.D. 35 until the early fourth century outlawed Christianity, labeling it as "strange and unlawful," "deadly," "wicked and unbridled," "new and harmful," "mysterious and opposed to

S. AGNES V.M.

light" and "hateful." Besides being condemned for disloyalty to their motherland, Christians were accused of atheism, of hatred toward mankind, of incest, infanticide and ritual cannibalism; likewise they were held responsible for all natural calamities, such as plagues, floods and famines. Periods of relative peace when they were able to practice their religion openly would be followed by intense political persecutions. In the first and second centuries when their brethren endured harrowing tortures and martyrdom for not renouncing their beliefs, Christians exposed themselves to considerable risk by retrieving the bodies of the dead and giving them a proper burial. There are thousands of early martyrs who were placed in unmarked loculi known only to those who interred them. By A.D. 150 celebrations of the Eucharist at the tombs of the martyrs were taking place and it was in the catacombs that Christians found the strength and support to endure the trials and persecutions by praying to God through the martyrs' intercession. To this day the Catholic and Orthodox churches still incorporate relics of martyrs on their church altars. They did not refer to their burial grounds as catacombs, but rather as *koimeteria,* Greek for "sleeping places." For the Christians death was considered merely a sleep before resurrection. Indeed, the rooms of the catacombs resemble vast dormitories with rows and rows of resting places. Most early Christians requested to be buried as near to the martyrs as possible.

As the catacombs grew in size, small churches were constructed over the entrances. In times of persecution when these churches were destroyed by the state, the Eucharist was celebrated in banquet rooms constructed inside the catacombs. Graves were respected and considered inviolate by pagan Romans. Therefore, even

Rome

in times of the worst persecutions, the catacombs were safe havens from government desecration and Christians were able to gather to celebrate their funeral rites and the anniversaries of the martyrs and the dead. They also felt free to decorate the walls with frescoes of Christian symbols and images of fish, anchors, doves and praying figures, attempting to bring the light of the Gospel into the dark and cold funeral chambers. Similar motifs are carved into tombs. While the art on pagan tombs reveals the anguish and sorrow of human loss, the most popular Christian theme is Christ raising Lazarus from the dead. The belief in the afterlife is displayed everywhere in these underground chambers. The pagan image of Orpheus's carrying a sheep on his shoulders was converted to the image of Christ as the Good Shepherd: "I am the good shepherd, and know my sheep, and am known of mine." (John 10.14) The fish is still a favorite Christian symbol, referencing the New Testament when Christ told his disciples he would make them fishers of men. To primitive Christians the Greek word for fish was written "ICHTHYS." This formed an acrostic, which was a typical classical style of poetry in which the letters of words were ordered to form a phrase: Iesus, CHristos, THeou, Yios, Soter means "Jesus Christ, Son of God, Savior." By sketching a fish, even the most illiterate and primitive Christian was able to state a fundamental article of faith. The age of martyrs is considered ended in A.D. 313 with the Edict of Milan, by which the emperors Constantine and Licinius gave freedom to the Church. The practice of Christianity became an open one and there was no longer a need for graves to be marked with cryptic symbols. More florid inscriptions were engraved on tombs using openly Christian phrases. Pope Damasus I (366–384) is credited with

repairing neglected tombs and graves of the
martyrs, adorning them with poetical epitaphs
inscribed in beautiful lettering. Several of his large
stone tablets have been preserved in their original
form or in fragments. It was at this point in time
that the catacombs became real shrines and cen-
ters of devotion, attracting Christian pilgrims
from every part of the empire.

More than fifty catacombs have been identified; many of them remain unexplored to this day. They lie in several levels ranging from twenty-two to sixty-five feet underground in a space of more than six hundred acres. The stairways to the subterranean walkways are claustrophobic, the passages being seven to ten feet tall and a yard wide. At this writing, five catacombs are open to the public:

Santa Domitilla—named for the Christian niece of the Emperor Domitian's sister. Originally part of her imperial family's cemetery and a pagan hypogeum, it has a room for funeral meals and a well. It is most notable for the underground Basilica of saints Nereus and Achilleus, the two servants who converted Domitilla to Christianity. There are hundreds of inscriptions and some of the earliest paintings of Jesus teaching his apostles, as well as an early scene of the Epiphany, the raising of Lazarus and a portrait of Saint Paul.

San Callisto is the largest catacomb, with more than thirteen miles of underground passages. Having five levels, it contains the crypt of

Rome

the popes where nine early popes are buried, as well as the tomb of Saint Cecilia, the patron saint of musicians. She was one of the earliest Christian martyrs, and her body was found incorrupt in 1599 and moved to a church. A marble statue of it was put in its place, lying on its side with the cut of the executioner's sword plainly visible. Among the hundreds of thousands of graves, it is the inscriptions of the common people that are the most compelling with their requests to the dead to pray for the living and the inscribed prayers from the living for the dead. Named for the third-century pope who was its caretaker, the largest section of San Callisto has yet to be explored.

San Sebastian is the only catacomb to have remained open through the centuries. Named for a young officer in the imperial household who was martyred, it was reputed to be the temporary resting place for saints Peter and Paul before they were reburied in their respective basilicas. This burial ground was originally pagan, from the time of Trajan. In the third century, during the persecution of Valerian, the Christians hid the relics of the two martyred apostles here where they remained for forty years. Ancient graffiti, still visible, invoke Peter and Paul for protection. So many Christians wanted to be buried near the remains of the two famous martyrs that the Christians eventually built a basilica over the entrance in the fourth century called Saints Apostoli. Five hundred years later, the Romans forgot that the apostles had ever been interred there and renamed the basilica for San Sebastian.

San Laurence is the burial place of the saint famous for being martyred by being grilled alive. St. Agnes, the church over this catacomb, attracts many pilgrims as it contains the shrine to the well-known second-century virgin and martyr.

Left page: Graffiti invocation to saints Peter and Paul from the catacomb of San Sebastian. The bodies of both apostles were hidden here during the persecution of Valerian. Center: Early carving of the Holy Family from the catacomb of San Sebastian. Early Christian art was virtually invented in the catacombs as a means of relaying Christ's message of eternal life.

Priscilla is the oldest and most important of all the catacombs. Taking its name from the mother of Senator Pudens in whose house Saint Peter found refuge, it contains the oldest known liturgical fresco of the Christian Church, the *Virgo Sacra,* or *Deo Dicata,* a dramatic image of the consecration of a Christian virgin. There is also clear evidence of the great reverence and veneration for the Mother of God in a second-century painting of Mary holding the infant Jesus to her breast while a prophet points to a star over her head. There is a Eucharistic painting of a priest's breaking bread and giving it to people sitting together at a table as well as a fourth-century painting of Our Lord giving the Christian law to Saint Peter with the inscription *"Dominus legem dat"* ("The Lord gives the law"). This fresco is considered as confirmation of the legitimacy of Peter as Christ's choice to lead his Church as pope. It was discovered in 1887 and like many of the ancient frescoes exposed to air has almost completely vanished.

More than any other shrine or pilgrimage site, the catacombs reinforce the Catholic faith by showing very real examples of the earliest Christians practicing the mass. Inscriptions confirm the Catholic doctrine of the Resurrection, the sacraments, the veneration of the Blessed Virgin and the primacy of the Apostolic See. They are the authentic archives of the primitive Church, filled with images and heartfelt written messages of the first Christians testifying to their faith and proving in their everyday life their fervent belief in the words of Christ. Here popes, members of imperial families, slaves and vegetable vendors are all buried together in one communal spirit.

With the barbarian invasions of the fifth century, relics of many of the martyrs were trans-

Graffiti inscriptions written on tiles sealing the loculi, or graves. The catacombs are filled with heartfelt messages invoking the dead to pray for the living and promises from the living to pray for the dead.

ferred to churches and burials were conducted in above-ground cemeteries. To protect the catacombs from marauding grave robbers, the entrances were sealed. In the course of time, landslides and vegetation hid all traces that they had ever existed. They were not rediscovered until 1578 and not fully explored until the nineteenth century by Giovanni Battista de Rossi, who discovered the existence of San Callisto. The preservation and maintenance of the catacombs are officially controlled by the Vatican state and archaeological work is ongoing.

Though a massive burial ground, the catacombs are a testament to eternal life. Thousands of pilgrims come from every corner of the world to experience what Saint Gregory the Great described as the "uproar of silence" and to witness the original messages of the first Christians that are contained here. As one of the many thousands of ancient graffiti wall writings states: "There is light in this darkness. There is music in these tombs."

Chartres

France

3

43

Chartres

France

Left page: Notre Dame de la Belle Verrière is one of the oldest and most famous stained-glass windows in the world. Dating from 1150, it survived the fire that destroyed the Romanesque cathedral. Made by master glaziers who have never been equaled in technique, it is considered worthy of a pilgrimage in itself. Right: Detail of sculptures carved into the royal portal between 1145 and 1170.

It is impossible to find a place with more reverence for the Virgin Mary than Chartres, France. The cathedral dedicated to her, Notre-Dame de Chartres, begun in 1195, is the epitome of Gothic architecture and is known as the jewel of France. Considered one of the greatest complete masterpieces of Europe, it has inspired a host of mystics, writers and artists. The great architectural and artistic innovations manifested in the building of this cathedral created a giant leap forward in the worlds of art and architecture. They were developed with a miraculous intuition inspired by adoration of the Mother of God, the patroness of Chartres.

The Druids, who were ancient Celtic priests, held their annual meeting to arbitrate private and intertribal disputes in the tree groves where the present-day cathedral stands. Religious ceremonies were performed in these groves because it was thought to be a place where spiritual energy emanated from the earth, giving the surrounding

area a mystical quality. In 100 B.C. the Druids received a revelation of the coming of a new order in which a virgin would bear a god king. An image of the goddess with an infant on her knees was carved into the trunk of a pear tree. This little statue was placed on an altar in a subterranean grotto. Known as the Virgo Paritura, or the Virgin Who Must Give Birth, it was considered by early Christians to be a premonitory image of the Virgin Mary. This statue, eventually known as the shrine of Notre-Dame de Sous-Terre, was kept in the church built over the grotto in the year A.D. 67 and served as a bridge between the old goddess religions and Christianity. Many churches have stood over this spot in the past two millennia. The current cathedral is considered the sixth church to have stood on this same hill and there are still traces of foundations from the fourth century.

In 876, the church received the relic that would make it a major pilgrimage stop, the veil of the Blessed Virgin. First given to Charlemagne, Crusader and emperor of the Franks, by the emperor and empress of Constantinople, it was transferred from Aachen Cathedral to Chartres by Charlemagne's grandson, Charles the Bald. This veil, also known as the Sancta Camisia, is purported to be the cloth the Virgin Mary was wearing when she gave birth to Christ. Commoners and kings began coming to the church at Chartres to see it, adding to the city's prosperity and fame. Chartres became a crossroads of learning with an important library and an international band of scholars. In 911, when the city was attacked by Norman invaders, the local people took the veil from the church and paraded it as a war flag. The Normans were defeated and the siege was lifted. This reinforced the very strong belief of the people of Chartres in the power of being under Mary's protection. In 1020, the wooden church was

Top: Chartres Cathedral with its Gothic and Romanesque towers. The Romanesque spire was completed in 1160 and survived the fire that destroyed the original cathedral. In the sixteenth century the north spire was hit by lightning and rebuilt. Right page: Working with the common goal of attaining the most height and light inspired master masons to develop the pointed arch, ribbed vault and flying buttress, which made it possible to support the weight of the massive structure.

replaced by a stone one, preserving the original crypt and the underground grotto. This structure was followed in 1120 by the construction of a new Romanesque-style cathedral. In the early Middle Ages most of the Carolingian kings and several English kings came to pray to the Virgin of Chartres. The collection of relics increased with the church's renown. The skull of Saint Anne, the mother of Mary, which had been looted by the Crusaders from Constantinople, was also bequeathed to the chapel.

The citizens of Chartres so adored the Virgin Mary that when the Romanesque cathedral was enlarged in 1145, all classes of society joined in the efforts to aid in the renovation. Known as the Cult of the Carts, the men of Chartres began to drag carts, harnessed to their shoulders, loaded with building supplies and other provisions needed for the expanded church. Others joined in, working in a friendly rivalry all in the service of the church and the Mother of God. A written account of this activity by a twelfth-century witness said, "When the towers seemed to be rising as if by magic, the faithful harnessed themselves to the carts . . . and dragged them from the quarry to the cathedral. The enthusiasm spread throughout France. Men and women came from afar carrying provisions for the workmen—wine, oil, corn. Among them were lords and ladies, pulling carts with the rest. There was perfect discipline and a most profound silence. All hearts were united and each man forgave his enemies."

The oldest parts of the present-day cathedral are from this Romanesque version of the church and include the royal portal, an area surrounding three doorways at the lower west front that was carved between 1145 and 1170. In 1194, the citizens of Chartres were devastated to find that the church that they had communally worked so hard to build was destroyed by fire. Despite this catastrophe, which destroyed all of the cathedral except for the Romanesque spire completed in 1160, the royal portal and a few stained-glass windows, the Sancta Camisia was found intact three days after the ashes had cooled. A papal delegate was able to convince the spiritually demoralized people of Chartres that this was a sign from the Virgin that they should rebuild an even larger, more magnificent cathedral on the same location. It was this next cathedral, begun because of a miraculous sign, that would revolutionize art and architecture.

In 1195, the new cathedral was started with the same communal spirit but on a grander scale—this time all of France and many parts of Europe contributed gifts for the rebuilding. Contributions flowed in from kings, the nobility and all ranks of the Church as well as from merchants, guilds, workmen and peasants. The building, which was completed in about 1222, was a turning point in Gothic architecture. The delicacy and soaring height of the cathedral were the result of a slow evolution in building techniques. Working with the common goal of attaining the most height and light, inspired master masons developed the pointed arch, ribbed vault and flying buttress, which made it possible to support the weight of the massive structure. Chartres is the first cathedral to make use of flying buttresses, which are arched projections attached to the exterior of a building. They transfer the weight away from the walls, allowing for more height and windows in the structure. Built of limestone, this cathedral stands 112 feet high and is 427 feet long.

The architectural sculptures at Chartres, which adorn the outside of the building and the porticoes of the doors, represent another artistic advancement. The carved figures reflect individu-

France

Left, top: Detail of the sixteenth-century clock pavilion. Left, bottom: Detail of an interior column. Right: The carved figures adorning the outside of the building reflect individualized characteristics, marking the beginning of a trend toward portraitlike carving.

alized characteristics marking the beginning of a trend toward portraitlike carving. Made in an era when the majority of the population was illiterate, they tell biblical stories with a sculptural grace not seen since classical Roman times.

With the exception of the carved altar screen there is no sculpture inside the cathedral, ensuring that nothing would deaden the acoustical resonance of the building. A column in the interior of the cathedral is clearly decorated with the twelve signs of the zodiac. This shows that many of the craftsmen and artisans who worked there were steeped in the traditions of pagan art, probably brought back from the East by the Crusaders. In 1200, the labyrinth known as The Road to Jerusalem was laid in the floor. One of the few labyrinths to survive from the Middle Ages, its four quadrants were meant to be walked as a pilgrimage or for repentance. The labyrinth, also known as a pavement maze, was walked by the devout as they meditated on becoming closer to God. Those serving a penance traveled the three hundred yards on their knees. The pattern for this particular labyrinth was first seen on Grecian coins minted in 300 B.C. and is known as the labyrinth of the Cretan Minotaur. Labyrinths were common in Gothic cathedrals but most were taken out and destroyed as the tradition of making a pilgrimage waned during the Reformation.

Perhaps the most incredible achievement of Chartres Cathedral is the creation of its stained-glass windows. Combined with the graceful Gothic architecture and the darkness of the interior masonry, they appear to be suspended in space, the entire cathedral serving as a framework for the glass. Most of these windows were made between 1215 and 1240. Because they could only calculate what the finished piece would look like from a distance with light shining through, the glaziers had to be expert and sure of their technique.

To this day, modern stained-glass artists cannot duplicate the famous Chartres blue, which pre-dominates in the images. Like the carvings on the outside of the building, the windows were meant to be educational, many of the subjects illustrating times in the life of the Virgin Mary. There are 176 windows covering an area of twenty-two thousand square feet. Five thousand figures represent scenes from the Bible and the lives of the saints. Subtle variations of color are produced by the continually changing outside sunlight. In dull weather, the colors take on a deeper, more mysterious hue and in sunny weather they acquire a sparkling radiance. Forty-two of the original windows were donated by merchants of the city and they offer insight into the range of occupations of the

The royal portal and details.

workers who took part in the cathedral's creation. In all there are the visual signatures of about seventy guilds proudly shown at their work. Underneath King David and Ezekiel is a butcher demonstrating how to kill an ox with an ax. The winemakers' window shows the use of wine at mass. The furriers gave the Charlemagne window, depicting the *Chanson de Roland*. Their signature is a furrier showing a fur-lined cloak to a client. Not only are these windows an example of great artistry, but their signatures are also visual examples of how society functioned in the Middle Ages.

The figure of Notre-Dame de la Belle Verrière (Our Lady of the Beautiful Glass) is considered worthy of a pilgrimage in itself. Dating from 1150, it not only survived the disastrous fire that destroyed the Romanesque cathedral, but its gemlike richness of colors and the placement of the blues and reds also give it an ethereal quality that has never been equaled in stained glass since. When the cathedral was rebuilt, Notre-Dame de la Belle Verrière was installed in the choir, where it is now the centerpiece of a large window, surrounded by thirteenth-century angels. It portrays a seven-foot-tall Virgin with the Christ child on her lap, his right hand raised in a blessing. His left

France

hand holds a book, showing a quotation from Isaiah: "Every valley shall be exalted."

During the Reign of Terror that followed the French Revolution, Chartres Cathedral was fortunate to be among the few houses of worship to escape violent destruction. While many of the ancient cathedrals had their exquisite windows smashed, Chartres is the only cathedral in France to carry an almost complete original set from the thirteenth century. The Druid statue of Notre Dame de Sous-Terre was not as lucky. It was desecrated and burned and was not replaced with a copy until the mid-nineteenth century. The Sancta Camisia was also cut into pieces and given out to all present. However, the cathedral was able to retain the largest part and this is what is in the reliquary today. It is processed through the town every year to honor the Feast of the Assumption on August 15.

The present-day cathedral at Chartres was consecrated in 1260. Improvements and changes were continually made on the building. In the sixteenth century the north spire was hit by lightning. It was rebuilt by Jean de Beauce along with the choir and the clock pavilion. The wooden roof frame burned in 1836 and was replaced by a metal roof whose green color brings out the beauty in the light-colored limestone façade.

Since the ancient days of the Druids, Chartres has been a pilgrimage center. The cathedral that stands today was built by workers who had submitted to a higher power that enabled them to surpass any building that had been constructed before it in human history. Whether to see a carved statue, a sacred cloth or a miraculous piece of architecture, those seeking the human face of God through Mary are drawn to Chartres Cathedral. It remains one of the highest architectural and artistic achievements ever accomplished by man.

Chimayó

4

New Mexico

Chimayó

One of the most revered Catholic sites in America is not an incredible cathedral or stadium-size church. Rather, it is a humble well of hallowed ground in the foothills of the Sangre de Cristo Mountains of northern New Mexico. Attracting well over three hundred thousand people a year, this tiny adobe sanctuary, which was built between 1814 and 1816, is believed to be a place of miracles. El Santuario de Chimayó, known as the Lourdes of America, is a place of utter peace that brings spiritual unity to the Tibetan Buddhists, Quakers, Sikhs, Sufis, Native American religious practitioners and Roman Catholics who flock there in search of spiritual and physical healing.

There is no written testimony for the story of the sanctuary. It has been traditionally handed down through the generations. In 1810, during Holy Week on the night of Good Friday, Don Bernardo Abeyta, a local landowner, was in the hills in Chimayó when he saw light emanating from the ground nearby. He started to dig up the lit ground with his hands, uncovering a crucifix with a dark Christ figure on it. Local people noticed its similarity to the miraculous figure of Our Lord of Esquipulas in Guatemala and gave it the same name. A group went to the priest in nearby Santa Cruz who upon hearing the news took his congregation, which was in worship at the time, to Chimayó where the crucifix was. They carried it back to the church in a procession and placed it on the altar. The next morning, it was missing from the church. After much searching,

Left page: Main altar painted by Molleno, a renowned ninteenth-century New Mexican folk artist. Center: Bulto of Saint James on a horse. Due to the difficulty of obtaining traditional European images in the eighteenth century, Spanish missionaries began carving and painting their own statues. This eventually evolved into a unique form of art in itself.

Top: Santo Niño Atocha is a very popular cult figure among the pilgrims to Chimayó. Local people believe that Santo Niño Atocha leaves the chapel and wanders the area at night on errands of mercy. Right page, top: Interior of the sanctuary. Center, top: The simple churchyard of the sanctuary. Center, bottom: Carved wooden door from the interior of the sanctuary.

the crucifix was found in the original hole in the ground. It was returned to the church from which it was missing again the next day. When this scenario was repeated a third time, the people decided that the cross wanted to remain in that spot in Chimayó, so a chapel was built over the mud hole where it was found. Because the cross was considered miraculous, pilgrims began coming from all over to see it. Eventually, it was discovered that the earth from the hole it was in had great healing powers and a larger church was built in 1816 to accommodate the increase in worshipers. Originally called Nuestro Señor de Esquipulas, this modest adobe mission is now known simply as El Santuario de Chimayó.

Long before the European settlers discovered the healing properties of the dirt around Chimayó, this land was considered sacred by the Tewa Indians. *Tsimayo* in the Tewa language means "good striking stone" (obsidian rock). They frequently used the ground of this area to make arrowheads, knives and tools. According to their legend, it was a place where fire, smoke and hot water existed together and it was also where a giant who devoured children was killed by twin war gods. After this, flames erupted from many places on the earth and the hot mud that was produced dried up and left the miracle earth of Chimayó. Shortly after the Pueblo Revolt (1680–92), when the Indian tribes drove the Spanish out of Santa Fe, several groups of Spanish colonists settled in the Chimayó Valley. They came to the area in hopes of receiving the title *hidalgo* (nobleman) if they succeeded in staying there. In exchange for their harsh existence on the frontier, they were granted land, building lots, subsidies and farming implements. In the archives from Durango, Mexico, there is mention of a priest from Guatemala who came to Chimayó with the origi-

nal settlers. He carried a large crucifix with him when he would minister to the surrounding Indians and pueblos. Eventually, he was killed by the Indians and buried with his cross at El Potrero. The Santa Cruz River flooded in 1810 and washed the grave away, exposing the body and the crucifix of the martyred priest. The older people remembered him and called him the Father from Esquipulas and the name became associated with the crucifix. Upon finding the cross, Don Bernardo Abeyta and nineteen other families of the El Potrero area got official permission to build the church that would become such a popular pilgrimage shrine. The church remained in private hands until 1929, when several people from Santa Fe purchased it from the Chavez family and donated it to the Archdiocese of Santa Fe. In 1970, El Santuario was designated as a national historic landmark.

Our Lord of Esquipulas, the original miraculous crucifix of the black Christ, was carved in 1595 at the request of the indigenous people of Esquipulas,

Guatemala. They wanted the image of the crucified Christ to have the same dark colored skin as they. Unfortunately, the sculptor could not find wood dark enough and they had to accept a carving with a much lighter coloration. They put the crucifix in a cabin hut until the shrine being built was finished. Miraculously, when they took the crucifix out to place it in the shrine, it had greatly darkened, turning the same color as the people.

This was a very popular story among both settlers and Indians throughout the Spanish settlements in the New World. Like the story of Our Lady of Guadalupe in Mexico, where the Virgin Mary appeared as a mixed-race Aztec/European woman, it illustrates that God held all the races of humanity on an equal footing. It is very likely that the cross carried by the dead priest on his rounds in Chimayó was a copy of Our Lord of Esquipulas and this is the same five-foot crucifix with its black Christ that still hangs over the main altar of the sanctuary.

This cross, which began the original shrine, has somehow been overshadowed by *el posito,* the sacred sand pit in which it was found. In the back of the church is a room with a hole in the floor where devotees dig up the holy dirt and put it in small plastic bags. Twenty tons a year are said to be taken by pilgrims. The soil is used for healing, and tradition has it that no matter how much soil is removed from it by the devout, *el posito* always remains filled. Those who have been cured leave behind the signs of the cures: crutches, hospital ID bracelets, eye patches, even a breathing tube line the left wall. *Milagros,* little metal stampings in the shape of parts of the body, decorate the chapel signifying miraculously healed arms, legs, hands and ears.

The rest of the small adobe church is decorated with sculptures and paintings of saints done in the traditional folk style unique to Mexican art. The

Exterior of the Sanctuary of Chimayó in the foothills of the Sangre de Cristo Mountains. A very simple building, it was constructed without using nails in 1816.

altar features a large gold screen, or reredos, decorated with paintings of various religious symbols. It was painted by Molleno, the "Chili Painter," one of the more famous artists of the 1800s. Due to the difficulty of obtaining religious devotional objects for churches and chapels in New Mexico during the eighteenth century, Spanish missionaries and artisans began making *santos,* carved and painted religious figures of saints, shortly after the reconquest. This created a whole new style of devotional art. The heartfelt simplicity of the many *bultos* (carvings) and painted depictions of saints in the interior of the sanctuary gives one the same spiritual feeling of the very early Christian holy sites of Greece and the Middle East. The sanctuary itself is a quaint, simply constructed and perfectly preserved adobe mission church, built without nails. It has twin square bell towers with a wide main portal and gallery-level covered porch reached by a doorway from the choir loft.

A favorite saint of the pilgrims who visit the sanctuary, as well as the people of New Mexico, is Santo Niño Atocha. There are several shrines ded-

icated to this depiction of Jesus as a child. Local people believe that Santo Niño Atocha leaves the chapel and wanders in the area at night on errands of mercy, often wearing out his shoes, so pilgrims bring baby shoes (or even pairs of tiny sneakers) as ex-voto offerings. The devotion to El Santo Niño Atocha originated in Spain in the thirteenth century when battles between Christians and Moors were commonplace. The Moors invaded the town of Atocha and held a great many Christians captive. They prevented adult visitors from bringing food or water to the prisoners. Fearing for the lives of their relatives, the townspeople bombarded heaven with prayers. The next day a child, dressed in the costume of a Santiago pilgrim, appeared carrying a basket of food and a gourd of water. The Moors allowed the child to bring these provisions to the prisoners every day. No matter how much the prisoners drank or ate, the basket and gourd remained full. Since the child was unknown to both Moors and Christians, the townspeople concluded that the child Jesus, disguised as a pilgrim, had come to their rescue. Santo Niño Atocha is a protector of travelers and pilgrims and is the patron saint of those unjustly imprisoned.

Because of the discovery of the crucifix on Good Friday, Holy Week is traditionally the busiest time to make a pilgrimage to El Santuario de Chimayó. Some years as many as sixty-five thousand people have come to pray and petition for favors during this time. Most make a three-hour walk from the town of Espanola joined by the archbishop of New Mexico, who makes this pilgrimage not as its leader but as just another pilgrim. Many carry physical burdens such as heavy crosses; others are handicapped and travel in wheelchairs. The New Mexico state police sees to it that objects are cleared along the shoulder of the highway for the safety of the pilgrims. By the morning of Good Friday, the

New Mexico

A view of the Good Friday pilgrimage to Chimayó. Some years this pilgrimage has attracted as many as sixty-five thousand people. A good number join in spontaneously along the way. Left page: Bulto of San Rafael Archangel. The interior of the sanctuary is totally decorated with these unique hand-carved figures.

church courtyard begins to fill up with worshipers, some walking from far greater distances than Espanola. So many people join the procession spontaneously along the way that every year there are a number of people who collapse from dehydration or need medical attention because they have worn the wrong types of shoes. For most pilgrims the Holy Week pilgrimage is a matter of tradition. They were brought by their parents and grandparents and are now bringing their own children. During the year, there are several other official pilgrimages, including one in June, a hundred-mile walk coming from two different directions. Countless travelers visit the shrine for healing during the year, flying in from all over the world.

El Santuario de Chimayó mirrors the unique cultural heritage of New Mexico. A mixture of indigenous Indian, Spanish and Anglo-American traditions, this Catholic church stands as a shrine of hope and healing to all. When the conquistadores arrived here five centuries ago, they were looking for gold and did not find it. What they *did* find was a world of spiritual riches in a place where the earth was truly blessed.

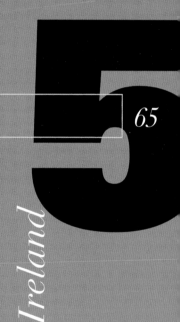

Lough Derg and
Croagh Patrick

Ireland

5

65

Lough Derg and Croagh Patrick

Left page: A Tiepolo painting of Saint Patrick, bishop of Ireland. His incredible powers over the elements of nature are credited to the fact that he prayed over one hundred times a day.

Ireland is a country known for its natural beauty, so it is fitting that its two most important holy places are not man-made architectural wonders, but rather a cave known as Patrick's Purgatory and a mountain peak named Croagh Patrick. Both of these locations are directly related to Ireland's patron saint, Patrick, and they have been attracting pilgrims for the past fifteen hundred years. Pilgrimages to Croagh Patrick and Lough Derg, the site of Patrick's Purgatory, are the only harsh penitential journeys left in Catholic practice that are similar to the rigorous difficulties commonly experienced by religious pilgrims in the Middle Ages. Saint Patrick was a man whose incredible powers over the elements were attributed to the fact that he prayed more than one hundred times a day. In homage to him, both pilgrimages utilize hours of mantralike praying.

Saint Patrick was born on the west coast of Great Britain of Roman-British parents. At the age of sixteen he was abducted by pirates and taken to Ireland, where he was sold into slavery. For six years he was forced to herd sheep, living under the direst conditions, subject to cold, wind, rain and hardship. In his *Confessio,* the story of his life, he wrote that this was when he began his regimen of constant prayer. He was able to escape due to a prophetic dream and eventually returned to his family. In gratitude for God's help he became a priest. In A.D. 432 another dream instructed him to return to Ireland and to work on the conversion of the people to Christianity.

Though he would have preferred to perfect his studies and remain in Britain, he surrendered to the guidance of the dream and put all his faith in God by returning to Ireland. Living there at a time when the Druid religion was in decline, he nonetheless had to compete with the wizardry of the Druid priests, winning many converts with the superior powers of his prayers. It was said that Saint Patrick could turn people into deer and day into night. He spent nearly thirty years traveling around the countryside, bringing Christianity to the local people and establishing churches and monastic foundations upon many sacred Druid sites. Saint Patrick's life as a former slave and fugitive taught him to trust God completely, and those living in similarly miserable circumstances have always identified with him. He died in the monastery of Saul, and his remains are buried with those of Saint Brigid in Ulster.

Lough Derg

Lough Derg means "red lake." On Station Island, one of the eleven islands in the rusty colored waters of the lake, is a sanctuary known as Saint Patrick's Purgatory. Its isolated location and eerie beauty made it a natural place for religious anchorites. According to legend, Saint Patrick frequently came to pray in solitude. At the entrance of a cave he heard voices of the dead speaking from the depths. On further inspection he realized he had found the entrance to purgatory. He drove the demons guarding the entrance of this cave out and was rewarded with a vision of the souls in purgatory enduring much suffering as they waited to be cleansed from sin and allowed into paradise.

According to *The Golden Legend*, an early history of the saints and the Church written in the thirteenth century, "...He preached throughout Ireland but with very meager results, so he

A Celtic cross in stone. Irish history is told with its ancient stoneworks—from the dolmens of the Druids to the stone beds of the early Christian hermits.

besought the Lord to show some sign that would terrify the people, and move them to repentance. He then did as the Lord commanded him, and in a certain place drew a large circle with a stick; and behold, the earth opened within the circle and a very deep, wide pit appeared. Then it was revealed to blessed Patrick that this was the place of Purgatory, that anyone who wished to go down into it would have no other penance to do and would endure no other Purgatory for his sins; but most would not come back from there, and those who did come back would have had to stay below from one morning to the next. There were indeed many who went into that pit who did not come out ...." The book then details the excruciating horrors, tortures and visions that befall a man named Nicholas who ventures into Patrick's Purgatory long after Patrick is dead.

From 1100 to 1500 the pilgrimage to Lough Derg was considered one of the harshest and most challenging, attracting adventurers from England,

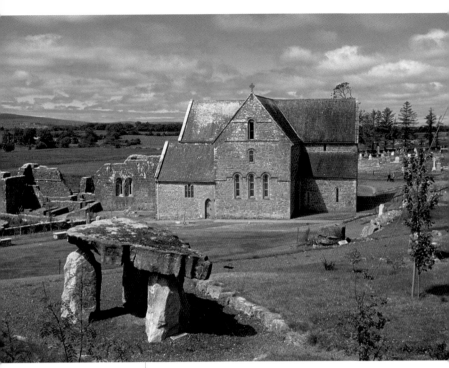

Ballintubber Abbey, at the foot of Croagh Patrick.

France, Italy, Hungary, Holland and Spain. They traveled to this remote land to self-inflict the experience of purgatory. After making the often treacherous journey, they would spend two weeks on the island performing penitential exercises of fasting and praying under the direction of an order of monks in charge of Lough Derg. When they were finally deemed ready to enter the cave they lay on the ground as the full Office of the Dead was chanted over them by monks. Sealed in the cave for twenty-four hours without food or water and after fasting for weeks, many reported having otherworldly experiences. Penitents reported falling into strange dreams, having odd visions and hearing the voices of the dead. Patrick's Purgatory became a subject in popular literature and pilgrims flocked to this holy place. It became popular for noblemen to come do penance for sins and atrocities committed during war.

In 1632, during the Reformation, the pilgrimages were banned by the ruling English government and the statues and relics in the little church on the island were smashed. This suppression was not successful as pilgrims continued to come, even if they could not get to the island, they could be seen standing on the shore's edge fasting and praying. The cave itself was sealed in 1780 and has never been reopened.

After the Catholic Emancipation of 1829, which permitted Catholics full liberty to practice their religion, the number of visitors to Lough Derg greatly increased. Today, twenty five thousand people per year take part in the pilgrimage to Lough Derg, from June 1 to August 15. The penitential exercises, though not as severe as in the Middle Ages, are still austere and harsh and the minimum age for a pilgrim is seventeen. Even in summer the weather is cool, damp and rainy and nights are frequently bitter.

The modern pilgrimage regime is three days long, not counting a day of fasting that must be done before arrival. The penitents remain barefoot and keep total silence at all times except for the reciting of group prayers. The pilgrimage exercises are made up of a prayer sequence called a station. This is a well-known Celtic form of prayer involving physical movement accompanied by the reciting of mantra-type prayers. Five of the nine stations are done around shrines in the open air. Pilgrims circle crosses honoring Saint Patrick, Saint Brigid, Saint Brendan and Saint Catherine. There are 1,449 prescribed prayers that pilgrims recite as they circle the basilica and the ancient stone penitential beds of the Celtic hermits who once inhabited this place. At night, the pilgrims enter the basilica for ritual closing of the doors, symbolizing the fearful hours that Saint Patrick spent fighting the demons in the cave. Inside the cathedral they pray all night, chanting 396 Our Fathers, 124 Apostles' Creeds and 648 Hail

Ireland

Marys. The constant repetition makes it almost impossible to let the mind stray from the words and their meanings as they echo through the consciousness. At dawn the pilgrims leave the church. There is one meal served of black tea and bread. The second day involves acts of reconciliation, the renewal of baptismal vows and making the different stations. These exercises and are drawn from the rich spirituality of the Celtic monks and few leave the island unchanged.

Croagh Patrick

Croagh Patrick is the holy mountain of Ireland. Located in County Mayo, its cone-shaped peak rises 2,510 feet over Clew Bay near the Atlantic Ocean. The pyramid-shaped reek, or cone, of the summit forms a spectacular landmark that is visible from many miles away. Beautiful at all times of the year, there is never a day when someone is not climbing Croagh Patrick. However, during the last Sunday in July (Garland Sunday or Reek Sunday) up to eighty thousand people have been known to

Ireland

make the trek up as an act of penance, in order to atone for their sins through physical sacrifice.

In Lent of A.D. 441, in obedience to his guardian angel, Saint Patrick made this mountain his hallowed retreat. In imitation of Christ's time in the desert, he spent forty days on its summit, fasting and praying. His only shelter from the fury of the elements was a cave or recess in the solid rock. The flagstone where he rested his exhausted limbs at night is still pointed out today. The whole purpose of his prayer was to obtain special blessings and mercy for the Irish people, whom he loved. When he rang his bell, all the snakes leaped from the crest of their mountain to their deaths. The demons that inhabited Ireland mustered all their strength attempting to distract the saint from his prayers. They gathered around the hill in the form of vast flocks of hideous crows, densely covering the whole mountain like a cloud. As they filled the sky Patrick could see neither sky nor earth nor ocean. Saint Patrick begged God to scatter the demons, but for a time it seemed as if his prayers and tears were in vain. In desperation he again rang his hand bell, symbol of his preaching of the divine truths. Its sound was heard all over the valleys and hills of Ireland, bringing peace and joy to every corner. The flocks of demons began to scatter. As he flung his bell at them, they took flight and hurled themselves into the ocean. Though he won this victory, the saint did not yet descend from the mountain or relax his penance. An angel came to comfort him. Saint Patrick still would not give up his post on the mountain and though exhausted would not stop praying. Again the angel came to him, this time delivering the message that Patrick's prayers had been heard:

—*Many souls would be free from the pains of purgatory through his intercession.*

—*Whoever in the spirit of penance would recite*

his hymn before death would attain heavenly reward.

—Barbarian hordes would never attain sway in his Church.

—Seven years before Judgment Day, the sea would spread over Ireland to save its people from the temptations and terrors of the Antichrist.

—Patrick himself would be the judge of the whole Irish people on the last day.

Today, following his example, pilgrims seek to expiate their sins or relieve the suffering of those in purgatory through physical suffering and sacrifice. Despite the sharp rocks that cover the hillside, many make the pilgrimage up Croagh Patrick barefoot or on their knees and by midday the path is marked with blood. They follow a series of stations up the mountain, several of which are stone beds, so called because of legends that saints once slept on them. The pilgrim circles each station seven times, reciting the Our Father, Hail Mary and Apostles' Creed. At the top of Croagh Patrick mass is celebrated continually, but before taking part, the pilgrims circle the small chapel there fifteen times. The last station is a cairn resembling a burial mound; it is circled seven times while praying seven Our Fathers, seven Hail Marys and one Apostles' Creed. Known as Roilig Mhuire (Virgin's Cemetery), this is a pre-Christian grave site dedicated to a pagan goddess. Even before it was renamed for the Virgin Mary, women came here asking for the favor of conceiving a child or to get a blessing for a child.

Long before there ever was a Christian religion, Croagh Patrick was a holy mountain to the Celtic people. It was called Croghan Aigle, or Eagle's Peak, until it was renamed on maps in the twelfth century. The mountain is ringed by old sites, monuments and standing stones that date back to 300 B.C. In fact, the traditional pilgrimage day on Croagh Patrick, the last Sunday in July, is the

Cairns like this one are an important part of the pilgrimage to Croagh Patrick.

Ireland

anniversary of the ancient Celtic observance in honor of Lugh, a pagan fertility god. The Festival of Lughnasa was celebrated all around Ireland and was vital for the success of the harvest. In many ways the pilgrimage to Croagh Patrick is the continuation of an ancient tradition.

There are many who say that Saint Patrick never had any affiliation with either Lough Derg or Croagh Patrick. But as recently as 1994, the remnants of a rude chapel called Teampall Phadraig was found on the summit of Croagh Patrick. It carbon dates back to the mid-fifth century. The bell he threw at the crows is in the National Museum in Dublin and there are still no snakes in Ireland.

Whether the legends that are attributed to Saint Patrick are true or not is of no real consequence today. What is irrefutable is that he has left a legacy of prayer that has created two more holy places in this world.

Lourdes

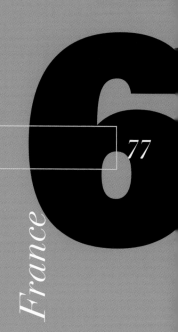

6

France

Lourdes

France

Lourdes, an ancient village in a valley of the Pyrenees Mountains, is in the extreme southwest of France near the Spanish border. It is the site of the most famous series of apparitions of the Virgin Mary and the most visited pilgrimage shrine in Christendom. Credited with exuding a powerful healing energy, it is inundated by those in need of physical and spiritual renewal. Attracting well over 200 million visitors since its discovery, Lourdes is a relatively modern holy site, having been recognized by the Church as an official pilgrimage place only in 1862. It became famous after a poor, illiterate, local fourteen-year-old girl, Bernadette Soubirous, saw a vision of the Virgin Mary in a grotto near a great rock mound called Massabielle. Despite the ridicule and persecution inflicted on her by the local authorities, Bernadette could not be shaken from her story. While communing with the Virgin, Bernadette uncovered a trickle of muddy water in a place where water had never been. Today, that tiny spring gushes forth with thousands of gallons of water daily. Considered to contain inexplicable healing properties by the devout, many terminally ill people of all faiths flock to Lourdes as a last resort in curing their ailments. Catholics go to spiritually refresh themselves and to honor this visitation by the Mother of God.

Though officially ruled over by France, the villagers of the Pyrenees had little to do with their country on any cultural or social level. Most spoke their own patois, never learning French at all.

Left page, top: The grotto at Lourdes where the Virgin Mary appeared to Bernadette Soubirous in 1858. Left page, bottom: A 1920s newspaper clipping depicting the pilgrims visiting the grotto for healings. Lourdes is still the most visited pilgrimage shrine in Christendom.

They dressed in local costumes, disdained the central government and were known as the Indians of France for the exotic way they lived. While the nineteenth century was celebrated as a great secular age, during which France was finally freed of political domination by the Catholic Church and science and logic replaced faith, the villagers of the Pyrenees defied all official teachings and held on to their religious beliefs. They were hostile to the French government and suspicious of any forms of official bureaucracy. Living in a harsh mountainous landscape, they held much of nature as sacred. They had little faith in modern medicine and combined ancient Celtic beliefs with their Catholic prayers. The love of the Virgin Mary was at the heart of their religious life. Since the thirteenth century shepherds and shepherdesses had reported direct contact with her, either through visions or the miraculous discovery of statues of her. Shrines to the Madonna were abundant and most towns had a special day of pilgrimage honoring her.

Bernadette Soubirous was a fourteen-year-old girl whose impoverished family lived in a dank former dungeon. Stricken with asthma, she was considered slow and held back from receiving her First Holy Communion because she had trouble learning her catechism. On February 11, 1858, her mother needed firewood for cooking and could not afford to buy any. She sent Bernadette, her younger sister and a friend out to look for some. So that they would not be accused of stealing, the girls had to go outside of town to public lands. There was an outcropping of rock facing the Gave de Pau River with a grotto at its base known as Massabielle. Not an area for respectable residents, this was considered a filthy place because pigs grazed there. According to legend, the Massabielle had been sacred to the pagans in prehistoric times and those passing by

Top: Today, the grotto, three churches and a basilica are encompassed in the Sanctuary of Our Lady of Lourdes. Left page: A French magazine illustration of one of the Virgin's visits with Bernadette. Bernadette never liked the artistic depictions of the Virgin of Lourdes, claiming they depicted Mary as "too big and too old."

it always crossed themselves to ward off the aura of evil that they felt emanated from it. Because of her illness, Bernadette stayed behind while the two younger girls waded across the river to get wood. She decided to join them and began taking off her stockings. It was at this point she heard the sound of wind and then saw a soft light coming from the niche in the grotto. A beautiful smiling girl in white seemed to beckon to her. Bernadette was startled and instinctively reached for her rosary. She was unable to pick it up until the young girl produced one herself. They made the sign of the cross together and as Bernadette prayed the rosary, the young girl passed her own beads through her fingers in silent prayer. When Bernadette finished, the young girl smiled and disappeared.

Despite her mother's opposition, Bernadette

returned to the site that Sunday after mass. She was joined by a group of friends. The girl in white appeared and Bernadette said, "If you come from God, stay. If you don't, go away." She then sprinkled holy water at the girl to make sure she was not from the devil. Bernadette was relieved when the girl laughed and inclined her head to receive more water. Bernadette was the only one who could see or commune with the girl. Her friends were astounded by the physical change in her demeanor. She had fallen into a beautiful rapture and seemed totally relieved of her asthma. One threw a large stone in the direction of the niche and Bernadette did not flinch. Fearing she had had some sort of fit, they ran to get help. The town's residents who came were shocked at the beautiful transformation in Bernadette. Word of her visions started to spread. Each time she returned to the grotto she was joined by a larger crowd.

Many thought the apparition was either the ghost of a devout townswoman who had recently died or a soul who had wandered away from purgatory. Bernadette's third vision was on February 18 and two important townswomen brought along a pen and paper. The girl in white laughed when Bernadette held out the writing instruments and for the first time spoke to her, addressing her with great politeness, *"Boulet aoue ra gracia de bie aci penden quinze dias?"* she asked in patois. ("Would you have the grace to come here for fifteen days?") When Bernadette replied that she would ask her parents' permission, the girl said, "I do not promise you happiness in this life, but in the next."

During these next two weeks news rapidly spread through Lourdes about the apparitions and the civil authorities felt obliged to take action. Bernadette was taken to the local police station for questioning. The authorities tried to make her admit that it was all a hoax. When she refused, they began to threaten her family. The Church was also skeptical and embarrassed by what they regarded as superstitious worship. The local pastor, Father Peyramale, did not want to give the apparitions any credence. Even though the girl in the visions had not named herself, the belief that she might be the Virgin was growing among the townspeople. For her part, Bernadette did not speculate on the mysterious girl's identity, always referring to her as *Aquero,* the patois word for indescribable being.

It was on February 25, during the ninth apparition of the girl, that Bernadette was told to go drink at the spring and wash in it. Thinking the girl meant the river, she went toward the Gave de Pau. In her words, ". . . *Aquero* called me back and pointed to a spot beneath the rock. I found some moisture there but it was mud. Three times I threw it away even though the Lady said to drink it. Then I washed in it only to have my face besmeared with mud. When the Lady left, my Aunt Bernarde slapped my face. 'Stop your nonsense,' she said as she sent me home to the jeers of the people." By the afternoon the muddy area was flowing with pure water and many in the laughing crowd were amazed, because they had never seen a spring there before.

In subsequent apparitions the girl asked for penitence and the conversion of sinners. Bernadette said that she was afraid that the people climbing all over the grotto would disturb the rosebush where the girl stood. "I was afraid she might fall, but she kept on smiling at the people. She loved them, and she always seemed sorry to leave them." At the thirteenth visit Bernadette was told to tell the priests to come to the grotto in procession and to build a chapel. Father Peyramale was enraged and told her that if the girl in white wanted a chapel she should say who she

France

was and she should make the wild rosebush in the niche blossom. It was after this thirteenth visit that the water in the spring was first accredited with healing properties. A pregnant woman with a paralyzed hand became totally cured and a stonecutter had his sight restored after he bathed his eyes in the water. Before this, there had been no physical proof of Bernadette's visits. The vast crowds that had started to accompany her did not see or hear the girl in white. They only believed in these visions because of Bernadette's great physical transformation.

Thursday, March 4, was the last of the fifteen days. More than eight thousand people went to the grotto expecting to see something miraculous. At the end of her vision, which lasted forty-five minutes, Bernadette put out her candle and went home. The rosebush did not bloom, the girl in white did not declare any message. Bernadette, unconcerned about the wild emotions she had aroused, went home content. For the next three weeks, Bernadette later wrote, "The people pestered me, the police watched me, and the public prosecutor almost crushed me." Then, on the night of March 24, she awoke with the familiar urge to return. On March 25, the day of the Annunciation, she returned to the grotto at five A.M. The girl in white appeared and Bernadette asked her four times to say who she was. "*Aquero* extended her hands towards the ground, swept them upwards to join them on her heart, raised her eyes, but not her head to Heaven, leaned tenderly towards me and said, '*Que soy era Immaculada Conceptiou.*' ('I am the Immaculate Conception.') She smiled at me. She disappeared. I was alone." Father Peyramale was astounded at this announcement. This expression meant nothing to a simple peasant girl like Bernadette. The Catholic tradition that Mary had been conceived

Carving of Saint Bernadette and Father Peyramale.

without original sin so that she might be worthy to be the Mother of God had only been formally defined as Church doctrine in 1854. Eventually, the parish priest would be Bernadette's greatest defender as she was harassed and examined by government officials, psychologists and Church hierarchy. She never altered the account of her story to any of them, "I do not ask you to believe; I only told you what I had seen." Three eminent Parisian doctors declared that she was mentally and emotionally sound but that she suffered from asthma. ("My mother could have told them that and saved them the trouble.")

Under increased pressure from the authorities, the grotto was closed off and anyone visiting it threatened with arrest. On July 16, Bernadette saw the girl in white for the last time. She knelt in the meadow on the far side of the river. ". . . I began my rosary and my Lady stood in the grotto smiling at me. It was the Feast of Our Lady of Mount Carmel. She looked more beautiful than I had ever seen her. This would be the last time I would see her on this earth. . . . She left heaven in my heart and it has been there ever since."

While Lourdes developed into a world-famous place of pilgrimage, Bernadette, disliking the attention her presence created, joined the Sisters of Charity at Nevers in 1866. Her novitiate was difficult and her health deteriorated. She never showed any interest in the miraculous healings promised by the water in the spring. Her insistence that the girl in white was no older than twelve was ignored and priestly experts stated that since Mary had to be between the ages of fifteen and seventeen at the time of the Annunciation, the official image of the apparition should depict her at that age. Bernadette never liked the statue that was erected in the grotto in 1864, declaring it "too big and too old." She died of tuberculosis in

1879. When her body was exhumed in 1908, it was found to be uncorrupted. She was recognized as a saint by the Catholic Church in 1933.

Gradually, the local officials had to relent and reopen the grotto to the public. The bishop accepted the apparitions and approved the shrine in 1862. After the railroad line was finished in 1866, pilgrims began arriving in the tens of thousands. After 1873, when incidents of healing at the spring began to be reported, the shrine rapidly developed an international reputation for having healing powers. Bathing pools filled with cold water piped from Bernadette's spring were created for visiting pilgrims. Much pressure was put on the scientific community to repudiate the healings at Lourdes. Many illnesses were declared to be hysterical in nature and therefore cured by the powers of suggestion. Studies of the water from the spring showed it had no special chemical properties.

In 1882, a medical bureau was established to test the validity of the cures. This bureau, the only one of its kind, is still operating today employing a very stringent criteria in its examination of alleged miraculous healings. Before a cure can be officially considered, a patient's medical records are studied by a commission of doctors and independent medical professionals. The alleged cure must be immediate and permanent to be regarded as a miracle. When an investigation does occur, the conclusion is placed in one of four possible categories: 1) There has been no cure. 2) A partial cure has taken place. 3) There has been a cure, but there are medical or psychological reasons for it. 4) There has been a cure for which there is no natural or scientific explanation. The pilgrim must then return after a year for further examination. Since March 1, 1858, the Church has recognized sixty-five miracles at Lourdes. There are countless undocumented healings and more than five

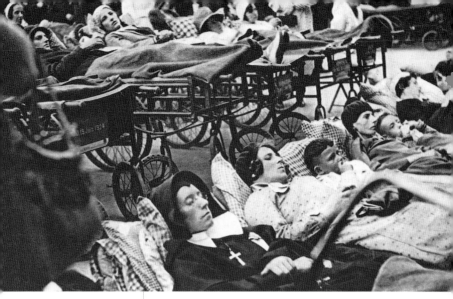

Since 1858, the Church
has recognized sixty-five
miracles at Lourdes.
There are countless
undocumented healings
and more than five
thousand documented
"inexplicable healings."

thousand documented "inexplicable healings."

Father Peyramale completed the first basilica upon the rock of Massabielle in 1873. After the great national French pilgrimages were initiated where Catholics of all classes came to bathe the sick at Lourdes, a larger church had to be built. The Church of the Holy Rosary was consecrated in 1901. Today, the grotto, three churches and a basilica are encompassed in the sanctuary of Our Lady of Lourdes. This includes a cavernous underground church, which seats twenty thousand. In the grotto the miraculous spring has been channeled into a long row of spigots where visitors may collect the Lourdes water and take it home. Three small hospitals and a number of hostels serve the needs of the seriously ill. There is a rosary procession held by torchlight each evening and the entire shrine is active throughout the day and evening with various services, processions and blessings of the sick.

At the heart of the Lourdes pilgrimage is service to the sick and the infirm. Many devotees do not go for themselves but to aid others and to commune with God in a holy atmosphere. There are four traditional gifts imparted by Lourdes: 1) The gift of miraculous water. 2) The gift of healing. 3) The gift of reconciliation. 4) The gift of strength and friendship.

Mont-Saint-Michel

7

89

France

Mont-Saint-Michel

7

France

Rising from the sea as if it were a mirage, Mont-Saint-Michel appears as a human challenge to the elements of nature and time. Perched on a summit on a rocky isle in the middle of a bay off the coast of Normandy, France, this spectacular sanctuary has been attracting pilgrims for almost thirteen hundred years. It is a UNESCO World Heritage site visited by more than 1.5 million people a year. Constructed over a period of more than five hundred years, it provides visitors with an overview of medieval architecture: pre-Romanesque, Romanesque and Gothic built in seemingly impossible circumstances. This isolated place of wonder has survived unscathed by sieges, wars, revolutions and acts of nature that have destroyed much of the surrounding area over the past thousand years. The protection and inspiration for this holy place is credited to Saint Michael the archangel, whose gold statue rises above the pinnacle of its highest tower.

Since he is considered heaven's defender and the greatest and most powerful of all angels, sanctuaries to Saint Michael are almost always founded on high rocky peaks where the divine may be in easy contact. He is cited in the Book of Revelation as the angel who defeated Lucifer in his uprising against God and is the only angel able to enter hell. From the earliest Christian times, the cults of devotion to Saint Michael were very popular, particularly in the East, where he was invoked against illness. As his popularity spread in the West, devotions to Saint Michael supplanted those to many of the pagan gods. In Germany, on the banks of the Rhine, he replaced Wotan, and in Roman Gaul, he replaced Mercury. Statues depicting an angel with a battle helmet and sword began to appear in such far-flung places as India and Persia. On May 8, 492, he was sighted in a cave on the summit of Mount Gargano in southern Italy. There he is credited with building a church and helping the Christian Apulians defeat the pagan

Previous pages, left: Interior view toward the choir. Granite blocks were hauled from the mainland during low tide to construct the abbey. Right: A view of the abbey at low tide. The tides surrounding the mount are the swiftest in France and the unwary pedestrian could easily be drowned by the sudden rushing waters of the tidal change.

France

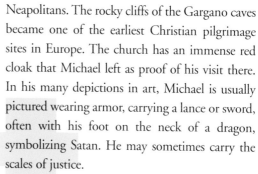

Left page: Sanctuaries to Saint Michael are almost always founded on high rocky peaks. He is considered heaven's defender and is the greatest and most powerful of the angels.

Neapolitans. The rocky cliffs of the Gargano caves became one of the earliest Christian pilgrimage sites in Europe. The church has an immense red cloak that Michael left as proof of his visit there. In his many depictions in art, Michael is usually pictured wearing armor, carrying a lance or sword, often with his foot on the neck of a dragon, symbolizing Satan. He may sometimes carry the scales of justice.

The Archangel Michael had three important tasks: 1) He weighed the souls of the dead in order to separate the damned from the elect. 2) He led the elected to heaven and protected them from any lurking demons. 3) He guarded the gates of paradise. High mountain peaks were considered the closest thing on earth to heaven; therefore, churches built on high points of land, called Michaelmounts, were dedicated to him.

In the beginning of the eighth century, Mont Tombe was situated in the middle of the Scissy forest, near Avranches, France. The Celts had worshiped their god Belanus on this mountaintop and the conquering Romans had built a shrine to Jove there. This region was known to be wild, poor and filled with dangerous animals. One night in 708, Aubert, the bishop of Avranches, had a dream in which the Archangel Michael came to him and said, "Aubert, devote Mont Tombe to me. I want you to build me a sanctuary like that on my Mount Gargano. I will make my residence there." Aubert, who was an overworked bishop and not a mystic, thought the very idea of building in such an impossible place to be completely crazy. He ignored the dream and again Michael came to him, demanding a sanctuary. Thinking this was all a figment of his imagination, Aubert ignored these orders. When he came to Aubert a third time, Michael was angry. In order to impress his point upon Aubert he poked him in the skull, leaving a gaping hole. This time, Aubert took the dream of the archangel seriously and had a small chapel built on the summit of the rock. Because they lived in such troubled and uncertain times, the faithful were quick to welcome the protection of the archangel and embrace his cult. The rock became a place of pilgrimage and Mont Tombe began to be known as Mont-Saint-Michel. In order to sanctify the church, two monks were sent to Gargano to get relics of Saint Michael. They received a small slab of marble on which the archangel had stood and a piece of the large red cloak he had left. This voyage took two years and many miracles were credited to these relics in their travels. By the time the two monks returned, the entire landscape and coastline of their region had changed. The forest of Scissy and the small coastal cities had disappeared. There remained only one immense white sand beach traversed by brooks, and isolated out in the sea stood Mont Tombe with the sanctuary to Saint Michael on it. They learned that in March 709, a great storm and earthquake had hit that region, flooding the area and separating the mountaintop from the mainland. According to Aubert, by devoting the top of Mont Tombe to Saint Michael he had enraged Satan. Realizing that he had forever lost another piece of influence on mankind, Satan put all his energy into trying to destroy the mount. When Aubert called on Saint Michael for protection, the forces of nature immediately became calm.

The sanctuary remained a modest place for several hundred years. In A.D. 966, Richard the Fearless, third duke of Normandy, installed the Benedictine monks from Monte Cassino in Mont-Saint-Michel. Under Abbot Hildebert II, a monastery, the first in this extraordinary scheme of buildings, was begun in 1017. Granite blocks were hauled from the mainland during low tide or

transported in boats, shaped at the base of the isle, then dragged to the top of the mount. The Romanesque abbey church, added in the eleventh century, was built over a succession of crypts on the very top of the island. In 1204, the Gothic cloister known as La Merveille (The Marvel) was begun. On the north side of the rock, facing the ocean, this vast structure is considered the most remarkable part of the mount as well as a masterpiece of Gothic architecture. Built in only sixteen years, La Merveille rises in three terraced levels with foundations 160 feet above sea level. The Hall of Knights, a uniquely arranged room with double arcades of columns, is considered the finest part of this structure. The cloister, built by Raoul de Villedieu, enabled the monks to meditate facing an immense landscape. The enormous refectory has narrow slit windows and thick walls supporting wooden barrel vaults. By using the natural rock of the island as a core and building around it, the structures on Mont-Saint-Michel are virtually invincible. A town eventually developed at the base of the abbey.

By 1421, the choir of the old Romanesque church had collapsed. A gigantic base called the Crypt of the Pillars was erected in 1446 to support the new choir. Appearing like stone trunks of colossal trees, these pillars give the illusion of a subterranean forest. In spite of collapses and fires and enormous difficulties involved in the design

When the early monks erected their church on the granite rock, they refrained from cutting away the pointed summit to keep from sacrificing about thirty feet in height. Instead, they took the peak as a level and built foundations all around it.

and construction of the sanctuary, its builders refused to waiver or be discouraged and persevered with a steadfast vision for five centuries. The sanctuary was completed in 1520 with the construction of the flamboyant choir.

While still a modest building, Mont-Saint-Michel had become a very popular pilgrimage site but pilgrims needed great faith to visit it. The tides surrounding the mount are the greatest and swiftest in France. High tide, which encircles the island twice a day, is fifteen feet higher than low tide. The unwary pedestrian could easily be drowned by the sudden onslaught of the rushing waters of the tidal change. Furthermore, the gray silt, or *tangue,* is constantly shifting, forming uncharted pockets of quicksand during the low tides. Due to the many dangers literally surrounding it, pilgrims referred to the site as The Mount in Peril from the Sea. During the Middle Ages spontaneous processions would gather and march to Mont-Saint-Michel. Thousands of men, women and children would amass and follow the "paths to heaven" that cut across France leading to the site. Walking through towns and villages and braving every sort of inclement weather was considered a small price to pay in order to visit what was truly one of the wonders of the world. The sight of Mont-Saint-Michel rising from the horizon was awe inspiring and beyond the imagination of the average person. Men went to Michael for protection in battle and medieval women went to him for protection in childbirth. When they arrived at the mount few were prepared for the mystical and mysterious atmosphere that it had. Watching the monks walking in moonlight processions intoning litanies against Satan made the presence of the archangel and his battle against evil very real.

Almost from its inception Mont-Saint-Michel enjoyed great support from the royalty of France. During the Hundred Years' War (1337–1453) between England and France, the French kings used the mount as a fortress against English attacks. The abbey and the little town that had grown up around it were enclosed by ramparts. Though most of France fell to the invading forces, the mount remained impregnable. In 1425, its 120 knights held off 8,000 English troops. News of this heroic defense spread through the French countryside giving hope to those loyal to the French king. It is believed that no one was more influenced by this story than Jeanne d'Arc. Many of her biographers attribute the dominant role of Saint Michael in her visions to be derived from hearing about the amazing defense of the fortress abbey.

The abbey flourished for centuries until it went into a decline at the end of the sixteenth century.

It was besieged during the religious wars of those times and in 1776 three western bays of the church were destroyed by a fire. After the French Revolution, the monks were dismissed and the abbey was secularized and turned into a prison. This practice was abolished by Napoleon III in 1863 and the French government took it over to be restored as a national landmark. Much of the statuary was found destroyed, the interiors looted of tapestries and art and many of the walls had fallen down because of neglect. A causeway was built in the late 1870s across the dangerous quicksand, making it easier to reach the abbey.

In 1966, to celebrate the thousandth anniversary of the monastery, the French government permitted the restoration of monastic life on Mont-Saint-Michel. Today, a small group of monks, nuns and lay oblates inhabit part of the abbey where they give tours and provide services to pilgrims. Mass is still celebrated daily in the abbey church and it remains an active parish for those who live on the island. Ex-votos, badges and petitions left by loyal devotees of Saint Michael can be found near a statue of the archangel, who is still considered an important spiritual ally by many pilgrims. Because of the famous visions of Saint Michael, there are local feast days to him on May 8 in Gargano and on October 16 in Mont-Saint-Michel. His official feast day is the Feast of the Archangel on September 29, which he shares with the archangels Gabriel and Raphael. On Mont-Saint-Michel this is when pilgrimages reach their peak.

Despite much turmoil in its thirteen hundred years of existence, Mont-Saint-Michel still survives in a magical atmosphere. The freak riptide that separated it from the mainland in A.D. 709 produced an ecological environment unlike any other place on earth. The bay around it brings together

A view of the abbey crypt. The Romanesque church, added in the eleventh century, was built over a succession of crypts.

a wide diversity of living creatures, a tremendous stretch of salt meadow, which, when not flooded at high tide, enables seven thousand sheep to graze there. Thousands of birds, shellfish and oysters inhabit the shore and a colony of brown seals regularly arrives for the winter. The amazing feats of the medieval architects and the power of nature and light have combined to make Mont-Saint-Michel a monument created with the best gifts of God and man.

St. Peter's Basilica

Italy

St. Peter's Basilica

Italy

Left page: A view of the statues on Bernini's colonnade with the dome of St. Peter's behind it. It was Michelangelo who finally solved the problem of how the building was going to bear the dome.
Right: A sixteenth-century rendering of the nave and side aisles of the early Constaninian Basilica of St. Peter's. This structure served the Christian community for twelve hundred years.

St. Peter's Basilica is the largest church in Christendom and is situated in an independent sovereign state, Vatican City, in the middle of Rome, Italy. It is considered the main church of Roman Catholicism, a symbol of the papacy and the tomb of Peter the apostle, honored by Catholics as the first pope. It took 120 years to build, engaging seventeen different architects and utilizing the talents of some of the greatest artists in history. This spectacular building was meant to be a tribute to the unity of Christianity, yet many blame its very construction for the schism that split apart Catholic Europe. Completed in 1626, it is the second basilica to stand on this site. Today, millions of people of all beliefs make a pilgrimage to it per year. Some come to view the artistic and architectural wonders it contains, others to pray in community with one another and

to pay respects to the first follower of Jesus Christ.

From the time that Peter the fisherman took his place as the head of the apostles, his character can be seen to evolve from an unpredictable and weak man with a violent nature to a charismatic leader able to effect miracles. The only apostle known to be married, he is described as being "uneducated and ordinary." It was Peter who sliced off the ear of the high priest's servant at the moment of the Lord's arrest, who fell asleep instead of keeping watch during Christ's agony in the garden and who denied knowing Jesus three times after insisting he would never denounce Him. Because there is so much written about

Italy

The vast forecourt of St. Peter's can easily hold three hundred thousand people. Designed by Bernini, it has the exact dimensions of the Roman Colosseum.

Peter, his spiritual journey, with all its doubts and impulsive acts, can be seen as mirroring the average man's and is easy to trace. For all his failings, Peter was the first to declare "Thou art Christ, the Son of the living God." To which Christ replied, "...Thou art Peter and upon this rock I will build my church...." After Pentecost, when the apostles were infused with the gifts of the Holy Spirit and the wisdom for future work, it is said that Peter converted three thousand people in one day.

Enduring the hardships of many travels, he suffered greatly for the early Church. He went on missions to Samaria, Joppa, Cesaria, Antioch and Corinth. He was imprisoned in Jerusalem under

Michelangelo's Pietà *is considered the most perfect sculpture ever made. It is one of many artistic treasures inside St. Peter's.*

the persecution of Herod Agrippa I and in a time of great danger established the early Church in Rome. When that city was badly damaged by fire in A.D. 64, rumors swept through the populace that the Emperor Nero was responsible. The great historian Tacitus, in explaining how Nero managed to deflect the charges leveled against him, documents the atmosphere of persecution Saint Peter and the early Christians lived in: ". . . Nero fastened the guilt and inflicted the most exquisite tortures on a class hated for their abominations, called Christians by the Romans. Christus, from whom the name had its origin, suffered the extreme penalty during the reign of Tiberius at the hands of one of our procurators, Pontius Pilate. But the deadly superstition, checked for a short time, broke out again, not only in Judea, the first source of the evil, but also in Rome, where all things hideous and shameful from every part of the world meet and become popular. Accordingly, an arrest was first made of all who confessed; then, upon their information, an immense multitude was convicted, not so much of the crime of arson as of hatred of the human race. Mockery of every sort was added to their deaths. Covered with the skins of beasts, they were torn by dogs and perished, or were nailed to crosses or were doomed to the flames. . ." According to tradition, Saint Peter was crucified with his head down in the Roman circus sometime between A.D. 64 and 69. As a condemned criminal, Peter, like Christ, did not merit a normal burial. The early Christians were known for secretly recovering the bodies of their dead and it has been recorded that Peter was buried in the public necropolis on Vatican Hill near the racetrack he was executed on.

The word *vatican* is a Latin derivative meaning prophecy and the Vaticanus Collis, or Vatican Hill, was a place where fortune-tellers would line up and offer their services to those passing by. On the right bank of the Tiber, it is not considered one of the seven hills of Rome. At the beginning of the first century, this was the site for the gardens of Agrippina. Her son, Caligula, built a racetrack there. Years later Emperor Nero was especially fond of this racetrack, or circus, and arranged countless spectacles in it, among them the martyrdom of the Christians. In part of the racetrack stood a plain obelisk without hieroglyphics brought from Heliopolis, the Egyptian city founded by the Pharaoh Ikhnaton, who also founded the first monotheistic religion. It was brought to Rome in A.D. 37 and is the only remaining remnant of Nero's circus. It stands today in the piazza of the Vatican, a surviving witness to the martyrdom of Saint Peter and countless early Christians.

In the year 323, Emperor Constantine had an immense basilica constructed over the cemetery and tomb of Saint Peter. It is hard to imagine what an amazing structure this must have been to the citizens of Constantine's empire. The nave was as long, as high and twice as wide as the nave of the great Gothic cathedrals built one thousand years later. Decorated with mosaics inside and out, it became the principal sanctuary of Western Christendom and pilgrims from all corners of the Earth began coming to Rome to pay tribute to the founder of the Church. Monasteries, churches and hospices for travelers soon developed in the area near the tomb of the "fisher of men." This early basilica was a magnificent achievement and it was known for its vast collection of art and treasures. Divided into five naves by four rows of twenty-two columns each, it expressed veneration for Christ through the wonder that being in such a space produced for the faithful. This incredible structure served the community of Christianity for twelve hundred years. When it began crumbling during the fifteenth century, plans were made to rebuild it.

During the years when the papal residence was moved to Avignon, the churches of Rome suffered from neglect. The decay of St. Peter's Basilica had progressed to such an extent that it was literally crumbling. Pope Nicholas V conceived of a plan of leveling the old church and erecting a new one in its place. Bernardo Rossellini of Florence developed plans for the new basilica to completely surround the choir and transept of the existing building and elongate the nave into a Latin cross. The tribune was begun in 1450 and the foundations of the walls surrounding the transept were dug, but work on this project stopped with the pope's death in 1455. Nothing more would be done toward building St. Peter's until Julius II's reign fifty years later. The architect Donato Bramante came up with a plan in line with the design of Constantine's basilica. Utilizing the Greek cross, it would be equal on all four sides, with raised ceilings and a huge dome similar to the Pantheon's. In the spring of 1506, Julius laid the foundations of this imposing structure, which, unbeknownst to him, would take more than one hundred years to realize. Under Bramante, much of the old church, which could have been preserved, was dismantled and destroyed. This earned him the nickname Bramante Ruinante. After his death in 1514, a parade of architects proceeded to work on the building. Giuliano da Sangallo and Fra Giacondo da Verona worked together with the artist Raphael to continue Bramante's plan. These two architects died in 1516 and 1515, respectively, and after the unexpected death of Raphael in 1520, a sharp conflict arose over whether the church should remain in the form of a Greek cross or have the nave extended to a Latin cross. Years of involvement from a myriad group of architects did

Italy

little to advance the project and it was not until Michelangelo took it over in 1548 that there was even the possibility of completion. He felt Bramante's original plan was the superior one and by strengthening the central piers of the building, he solved the problem of how it was going to bear the dome. One of the most sublime achievements in all of architecture, the dome was not completed during Michelangelo's lifetime.

His assistant Giacomo della Porta, faithfully following his master's plans, is credited with overseeing the dome's completion. It is generally agreed upon by architectural scholars that if these original designs had been followed per Michelangelo's intention, St. Peter's Basilica would have been the most perfect example of Renaissance architecture in existence.

The building would have been completed in the beginning of the seventeenth century if in 1606 the plans had not changed yet again. Pope Paul V decided to elongate the building in the form of a Latin cross. During the twenty years that followed, Carlo Maderno constructed the present façade and the new St. Peter's Basilica was dedicated on November 18, 1626.

The architectural aesthetics of the construction of St. Peter's Basilica were not the only controversy surrounding it. In order to raise the enormous sums of money needed for the construction, the granting of indulgences was authorized to contributors. In Catholic teaching, indulgences, the relief from punishment sinners endure after death in order to be purified for heaven, are normally gained by prayer or sacrifice. The idea of selling them for money horrified many throughout Europe and sparked a great scandal. This caused the German monk Martin Luther to challenge the very authority of the Church and that started the Protestant Reformation.

Despite the scandals, corruption and artistic disagreements involved in its creation, St. Peter's Basilica remains one of the most visited and welcoming places for the religious pilgrim. Its vast forecourt plaza can easily hold and embrace three hundred thousand of the faithful gathered together in prayer. Designed by Bernini, this open space, surrounded by 284 columns and statues of 140 saints, has almost the exact dimensions of the Roman Colosseum. The soaring interior contains

Italy

The center aisle toward the high altar, where only the pope may say mass.

some of the most famous works of art in the world, among them Giotto's 1298 mosaic of Christ's walking on water, which was saved from the old basilica, and Michelangelo's *Pieta,* considered the most perfect sculpture ever made. There are five sets of bronze doors leading into the basilica. One, the Holy Door, is opened only during holy years. Though this building was completed in 1626, the relics, memorials, artwork and architectural embellishments are from every year of the

Left page: A detail of the dome, which is 325 feet high and 138 feet in diameter. Under it is Bernini's baldachino, or canopy. It was commissioned by Urban VII in gratitude for the safe delivery of a favorite niece from a dangerous pregnancy.

Italy

Church's existence. The four massive piers supporting the dome are graced by statues of saints associated with the basilica's most treasured relics: the spear of Longinus, which was driven through the side of Christ; a piece of the true cross brought back from Jerusalem by Saint Helena in the fourth century; the veil of Veronica with the image of Christ imprinted on the handkerchief; and Saint Andrew, whose head was returned to the Greek Orthodox Church in Patras, Greece. The upper balconies are adorned with a pair of columns brought from Byzantium by Constantine for the original St. Peter's Basilica. The high altar, where only the pope may celebrate mass, is formed from a block of Greek marble found in the Forum of Nerva. It covers the altar of Calixtus II (died 1124) that in turn encloses the altar of Gregory the Great (died 604). It is sheltered by Bernini's celebrated baldachino, or canopy (1633), cast from the bronze taken from the roof of the Pantheon. The canopy is ninety-five feet tall and resembles the baldachino of the old St. Peter's. Decorated with seven heads of women in labor and one happy baby's face, this massive structure is possibly the largest ex-voto ever made. It was commissioned by Urban VII in gratitude for the safe deliverance of a favorite niece from a dangerous pregnancy.

The great dome is 325 feet high and 138 feet in diameter with sixteen windows, creating the effect of light moving upward toward heaven. In letters seven feet high is the Latin text of Jesus' prophecy to Peter: "Thou art Peter and upon this rock I will build my church and I will give you the keys to the kingdom of heaven." Also designed by Bernini is the black, gilt and bronze throne that was built to protect the original chair of Saint Peter behind it. This chair was believed used by Peter when he first came to Rome. It functioned

Italy

as a portable throne for the early popes and in 1656 it was placed in an inaccessible area to protect it from relic hunters. For centuries one of the most popular memorials in the basilica has been the statue of a seated Saint Peter as pope. Pilgrims have kissed its foot so often that much of it is worn away.

The scale of this building is overwhelming and it is made even more amazing with the realization that the entire placement of this structure was determined by the humble grave in the grottoes under the building. In 1941, excavators working in the basement of St. Peter's discovered a street of ancient tombs some three hundred feet long. This ancient necropolis had been filled in and the remnants of Constantine's basilica could be seen transversing the graves. The excavators had discovered that the street of tombs ran directly under the great altar and that great trouble had been taken to lay the foundations in this place. Further inspection revealed the red walls of a monument shrine with the words "Peter, pray to Jesus Christ for the holy men buried near your body" scratched into it.

The headless bones of an elderly, strongly built man were discovered in a niche. Scientific testing on these bones verified they were indeed from the first century. It has been recorded that the heads of both Saint Peter and Saint Paul were moved to the Church of St. John Lateran in the ninth century. Therefore, after years of only speculating that the basilica was built over the tomb of Saint Peter, this was declared to be true by Pope Paul VI.

Though a simple man, through his dedication and his love of Christ, Saint Peter, the most human of the apostles, inspired this basilica. Not only is it an architectural wonder filled with priceless works of art, but it also serves as an example of the endurance of faith for all who come to visit the tomb of the man Christ entrusted with leading his Church.

Santiago de Compostela

9

Spain

Santiago de Compostela

Spain

In the early ninth century a hermit in Galicia, Spain, was led by a vision of a star to a field. There he discovered the forgotten tomb of the apostle Saint James the Greater. The relics were authenticated and a small church was built. After more than one thousand years, though the little church is now a grand cathedral, pilgrims are still traveling throughout Europe by foot on a path known as el camino Santiago, the Way of Saint James, to pay homage to the patron saint of Spain. During the Middle Ages this pilgrimage was considered by Catholics to be third in importance to journeys to Jerusalem and Rome, attracting between 500,000 and 2 million devotees per year. Kings, popes and saints such as Francis of Assisi have made this arduous trek as well as criminals, merchants and families of all social strata.

Iago is the Spanish form of *James;* therefore, *Santiago* means *Saint James.* Saint James was a fisherman who, with his brother John, left his nets to become the first of the twelve apostles to follow Christ. Since they were Christ's cousins, they were considered the closest to Him and witnessed many of His first miracles. There are two apostles named James and he is known as James the Greater because he was with Christ for a longer amount of time. After Christ's ascension into heaven, the apostles had been bidden to spread out across the known world evangelizing the word of God. According to legend, the Iberian Peninsula was assigned to James the Greater. He had little success preaching to the Roman settlements in the north-

Left page: Portion of a carving of Christ and his twelve apostles. Saint James, the patron of Spain, is depicted in the standard pilgrim's garb from the Middle Ages.

west of Spain. After gaining eight converts in Zaragoza he saw a vision of the Virgin Mary (who was still alive at the time) held aloft on a throne by singing angels near a jasper pillar. She directed James to behold the pillar and build a church upon the site, promising him that Zaragoza would never lack for Christians. She gave him a wooden statue of herself with the Christ child, and Saint James built the first church dedicated to the Virgin Mary. He then returned to Jerusalem to continue his evangelization.

Because of his great success in making Christian converts, he was executed by King Herod Agrippa I in A.D. 44. James was the first of the twelve apostles to be martyred and the only one whose death is mentioned in the New Testament. His body was thrown outside of the city walls to be eaten by animals. Loyal Christians retrieved it and took it to the coast, placing it in a stone boat. This boat was carried by the wind, past the Pillars of Hercules (the Straits of Gibraltar) to land near Cape Finisterre, at Padrón, on the Atlantic coast of northern Spain. The queen of the region, Lupa, a pagan vehemently opposed to Christianity, was eventually converted by several miraculous occurrences surrounding the body. Saint James was respectfully buried inland on a hillside and the site of his tomb was forgotten for the next eight hundred years.

In the early part of the ninth century a hermit named Pelayo had a vision in which he saw a very large bright star surrounded by a ring of smaller ones, shining over a deserted spot in the hills. A tomb was discovered there containing three bodies. They were immediately identified as the remains of Saint James and two of his followers. Alfonso II, King of Asturias (791–824), declared Saint James the patron saint of Spain. He built a church and a small monastery over the tomb and the city of

The Cathedral of Santiago de Compostela. Construction on this building was completed in the thirteenth century. A Baroque façade was added in 1750.

Santiago de Compostela grew up around it. *Campus de la stellae* is Latin for "field of stars." At the time, Spain had been overrun by Muslim invaders and was badly in need of a champion of Christianity to defend its culture. In A.D. 844 in the Ebro Valley during the Battle of Clavijo, Saint James appeared in the sky on a white charger and led the attack against the Moors.

He was known thereafter as Santiago Matamoros, James the Moor Slayer, and his patronage is credited with the eventual reconquest of Spain by Christians. Many leaders felt compelled to visit the relics of Saint James to invoke him for protection. Gradually people from all different realms of life came to request favors and seek graces. By A.D. 1078, the Turks had seized the Church of the Holy Sepulchre, putting a stop to the pilgrimage to Jerusalem. This helped establish the popularity of the pilgrimage to Santiago de Compostela.

Santiago Matamoros (Saint James the Moor Slayer) is credited with inspiring the liberation of the Iberian Peninsula from Muslim occupation. Saint James is often depicted in pilgrim's garb on a white charger. Right page: Baroque interior of the Cathedral of Santiago de Compostela.

Spain

Pilgrimages are a feature of many religions and cultures. Christian pilgrimages began almost immediately after the ascension of Christ. The first Christians would visit the holy places of Jerusalem, Bethlehem and Nazareth. Gradually, the papal shrine in Rome, sacred to Saint Peter, Saint Paul and the martyrs, became an established site. Since the advent of Christianity it was believed that to visit a saint's shrine was no different from actually visiting a living person. The touching of relics was thought to ensure luck and physical well-being. The average citizen of the Middle Ages led a monotonous and hopeless life. On a daily basis they were reminded of the threats of hell and damnation through church sermons as well as through the carvings of the Apocalypse on the tympanum at the top of every village church. Embarking on a pilgrimage was not only a form of ensuring divine graces but also a way to relieve everyday drudgery. Many went on pilgrimages to fulfill a vow or to give thanks for a favor granted. Pilgrims were also rewarded for their efforts by the rest of society. While he was on a pilgrimage he was exempt from all taxes and lawsuits for debts. Criminals could work out their salvation by going on a pilgrimage dressed as beggars. Because a pilgrimage on foot often brings insight, even today judges will send juvenile delinquents out on the Way of Saint James.

Medieval pilgrims wore a special cloak and a broad-brimmed hat and carried a walking staff with an attached water gourd. Because of Saint James's miraculous return by sea, the symbol of Santiago is a scallop or cockle shell. Many tombs throughout Europe have this symbol carved on them, denoting the completion of a successful pilgrimage. Galicia is considered the oldest part of Spain, having been inhabited since prehistoric times. In 1000 B.C., it was settled by the Celts and

even today, the general population has retained physical characteristics close to the Irish. The land itself is lush and green, very different from the rest of Spain. Since the Romans referred to the Celts as Gauls, the area was referred to as Galicia. While the culture of most of the Iberian Peninsula was heavily influenced by the Arab invasion, because of the traffic in European pilgrims, Galicia stood apart and remained Spain's most European region.

The four medieval routes that led to Santiago began in France from Vezélay, Paris, Le Puy and Arles. Pilgrims from outside of France assembled at one of these points or joined the British, who sailed to Bordeaux. Starting in the foothills of the Pyrenees, the Way of Saint James is six hundred miles long. Though some of it is now paved, it is still a footpath, crossing the same fields, streams and mountain passes and visiting the same chapels, churches and shrines as it did one thousand years ago. Monasteries were founded along the way by religious orders to care for travelers and many of these, dating from medieval times, are still in use. A military order of monks, the Knights of Saint James, was established to fight the Muslims and provide security patrols for the pilgrims who followed the way. Though the wealthy could ride by horseback, the average pilgrim traveled by foot in a long and hazardous journey, menaced by wolf packs, bandits and inclement weather, taking about three months to complete the journey. Because of the need for shelter, the Way of Saint James runs through a variety of small villages and towns. Some of these ancient places are rich in art and architectural masterpieces, and they were crucial in providing a channel for intellectual exchange. The spread of the Romanesque style of art is attributed to the thousands of artists and craftsmen who traveled the way.

The route to Santiago was originally a Roman trade route. Centuries before the pilgrimages began, it was nicknamed *"la voje ladee"* (the Milky Way) by travelers. In almost all civilizations, from the Incas to the Celts, the Milky Way symbolizes a passage linking earthly reality with the eternal paradise. On the Way of Saint James, the Milky Way points to the westerly direction to the shrine. Upon entering the town of Santiago, it was customary for the first in a group who saw the shrine's towers to shout out, *"Mon joie!"* (My joy!), giving the hill across from the shrine its name of Mount Joy. In the Middle Ages pilgrims donned new garments, burning their filthy traveling clothes in a brazier on one of the towers.

After reaching Santiago de Compostela it was then obligatory to visit the chapel of Nuestra Señora at Finisterre, the last finger of earth over the ocean. This was, to the average man in the Middle Ages, the end of the world. The concept of the sacredness of certain places predates Christianity and it is possible that the Way of Saint

Spain

James was a religious pilgrimage route before the advent of Christianity. Many of the churches and cathedrals along the way were built in the same places as the sacred dolmens of the Celts.

The documents proving that one has completed the entire journey are the same today as they were in the Middle Ages. A pilgrim is given a passport at the starting point and has it stamped at all the way stations along the route. Pilgrims still have their passports certified before entering the great doors of the cathedral

The cathedral of Santiago de Compostela replaced the original sanctuary, which was destroyed by the Moors. Construction on the present building began around 1070 and was completed in the thirteenth century in the Romanesque style. A new façade was designed by the architect Casas y Novoa and its west front was refaced between 1738 and 1750 in the Baroque style, incorporating the nine towers of the medieval building. The Portico de la Gloria by the master Mateo is considered to be the most important monument of medieval sculpture. Completed in 1188, it is such a complex carving that it would take weeks to see all the nuance it contains. Side doors depicting purgatory and the Last Judgment flank the main door, which is surmounted by Christ's presiding over the apostles and elders of the Apocalypse as well as Saint James himself, in the role of intercessor. Supporting him is the Tree of Life. The pilgrims gave thanks at their journey's end with the fingers of one hand pressed on the roots of this tree. So many millions have performed this act of piety that five deep shiny holes have been worn into the solid marble. Inside, the cathedral is filled with Baroque carvings and beautiful side chapels. Marble pillars are worn smooth by the caresses of so many hands. It is customary for pilgrims to touch their heads to a column with

Spain

Tepeyac

Mexico

10

Tepeyac

Mexico

On December 9, 1531, a Mexican-Indian peasant named Juan Diego was walking through the countryside that was to become Mexico City. From the top of a hill named Tepeyac, a beautiful woman called gently out to him in the Aztec language of Nahuatl. When he stopped to see what she wanted, she told him she was Mary, Mother of God, and that she would like a church to be built upon the ground where she stood. She sent him off to the bishop to make the request. The bishop, upon hearing Juan's story, instructed him to obtain a sign to prove that this was truly an apparition of Mary. Juan, returning to the site, found the woman waiting for him. He begged her to get someone of a higher social standing to do her bidding, someone important whom the bishop would take more seriously. The Blessed Virgin answered, "Listen, my youngest child, you must understand that I have many servants and mes-

Left page: Altar inside the Templo de Cerrito, a church built on the top of Tepeyac in Mexico City. It is the site of the apparition of Our Lady of Guadalupe and the place where Juan Diego gathered the flowers. Right, bottom: A fresco inside the Templo de Cerrito depicting Our Lady of Guadalupe and Juan Diego.

sengers to whom I could entrust the delivery of my message, and carry my wish, but it is of precise detail that you yourself solicit and assist and that through your mediation my wish be complied." Again, she told him that she urgently desired a church to be built to bear witness to her love, compassion, help and protection. Once again Juan Diego went to the bishop and once again he was greeted with suspicion. When Juan Diego had gone, the bishop sent some of his trusted servants to spy on where Juan Diego went and whom he spoke with. But as soon as Juan Diego crossed the

Views of the old Basilica of Our Lady of Guadalupe in Mexico City. A new basilica was built in 1976 with the capacity to hold ten thousand people.

Candles, ex-votos and thank-you cards on the walls of buildings outside of the basilica. The Mexican people consider Our Lady of Guadalupe to be a very live presence in their lives.

wooden bridge to Tepeyac, they lost sight of him. No matter how hard they searched, they couldn't find him. When the servants returned to the bishop, they told him Juan Diego was a liar and that if he ever showed up at the palace again, they would teach him a lesson.

The next day, a Monday, Juan Diego did not return to the hill because his uncle Juan Bernadino was dying and needed a priest to hear his confession. Juan Diego thought it best to go around the hill so that the Virgin Mary would not see him and then ask him to take a sign to the bishop. "I'll go get the priest first," he said to himself. "My uncle can't just lie there waiting." So he went around the hill and came out on the east side to avoid being detained by the heavenly noblewoman. She came down the hill to meet him from where she was watching. "What is happening, dearest and youngest of my sons? Where are you going?" she asked. Juan Diego mournfully told her of his predicament and promised to return and do whatever she asked as soon as he brought a priest to hear his uncle's confession. At that Mary said, "Listen, put it into your heart, youngest and dearest son, nothing should scare or concern you. Don't worry. Don't be afraid of the sickness, or any

other illness or hardship. Am I not right here who is your mother? Are you not under my shadow and protection? Am I not in the foundation of your being, your sustenance, your happiness, peace and effortlessness? Are you not in the fold of my garment? Do you need anything else? Don't allow anything to worry or disturb you anymore. Don't worry about your uncle's illness. He will not die. Be assured, he is already well."

She then instructed Juan to gather roses among the rocks for the bishop. Since it was winter, not a season when roses bloomed, he was surprised to find them growing where she told him to look. After gathering the roses in his peasant cloak, he presented them to Mary, who arranged them; then he took them back to the bishop. After being forced to wait by the servants, Juan Diego was finally allowed to see the bishop one last time. As he unwrapped his cloak and the roses fell out, the bishop was stunned. The roses uncovered an elaborate portrait of the Virgin Mary imprinted on the cloak. When the bishop saw the image, he and all who were present fell to their knees. With sorrowful tears the bishop begged forgiveness and had Juan Diego show him where the lady from heaven wanted her temple. As soon as he had done this,

Mexico

Juan Diego asked to leave to be with his gravely ill uncle. A number of people went with him to his house. Upon arriving, they saw that the uncle was well, happy and healthy. Juan Bernadino then revealed that the heavenly lady had visited him and restored him to health. She also told him that as soon as he saw the bishop he must reveal the miraculous manner in which she had effected his cure and that he should convey to him the proper name for her blessed image: The Perfect Virgin Holy Mary of Guadalupe.

The bishop had the holy image of Mary on the cloak installed in the church so that all the people could see and admire it. He immediately began work on a church honoring Mary on Tepeyac, where the cloth could be seen by a large number of people. This poor-quality cactus cloth should have deteriorated in twenty years but shows no sign of decay nearly five hundred years later and its beautiful and clear image still defies all scientific explanations of its origins. This cloth is on view in the Basilica of Our Lady of Guadalupe in Mexico City. It attracts more than 10 million pilgrims a year, making it the most popular Marian shrine in the world. It is important to note that this apparition occurred ten years after the Spanish conquest of Mexico, on a hill where a temple to the Aztec corn and earth goddess, Tonantzin, once stood. The name Tonantzin means "our mother" and this is exactly how Mary asked the people of Mexico to perceive her. She wanted the world to know that she was a merciful mother to all and desired everyone to trust in her and invoke her in times of need This is the only apparition of Mary on the North American continent that is officially recognized by the Church. This makes Our Lady of Guadalupe not only the patron saint of Mexico but also the patron saint of the United States and the rest of the Americas as well.

A simple altar in the old basilica. The iconography of the image of Our Lady of Guadalupe appealed to both Europeans and Aztecs on two different levels.

When the Virgin appeared to Juan Bernardino, the sick uncle of Juan Diego, it is very likely that the name she called herself was misinterpreted by the Spanish as "Our Lady of Guadalupe." "Guadalupe" was not an easy word for Indians to pronounce and the Spaniards had much trouble with Aztec words. There are similar-sounding Nahuatl names and it is suggested by scholars that she could have used the name Tlecuauhtlacupeuh, meaning "She who comes flying from the light like an eagle." To the Aztecs, an eagle is a sign from the gods and the region of light is where the gods live. The name Our Lady of Guadalupe was not officially designated by the Catholic Church until 1566.

Extremadura, the province in Spain where Guadalupe is located, is where many of the conquistadores, including Hernán Cortés, came from. The word "Guadalupe" is a corruption of Arabic, meaning *"rio de amor, rio de luz"* ("river of love, river of light"). There is a shrine containing a black wood carved statue of the Virgin Mary that is said to have been carved by Saint Luke. During Spain's seven-hundred-year occupation by Muslim forces, this shrine was visited by many Spanish pilgrims

in an appeal to liberate and unify their homeland. Kings came to it to give thanks for successful battles against the Moorish invaders. Queen Isabella and her husband, King Ferdinand II, financiers of Cortés's expedition, were great devotees of this shrine (as were Cortés and many of his men) and frequently visited it in times of trouble. Cortés had sailed for the New World with a copy of this statue. Catholicism was credited for the national liberation of the Iberian Peninsula and was closely entwined with Spanish culture. This was why the conquistadores were especially fierce in their Catholic beliefs and considered religious conversion as one of their main tasks in the New World.

In 1519, Hernán Cortés landed in Mexico. Within two years his small army succeeded in leveling the capital city of the Aztec empire. By 1524, when the first twelve Franciscans arrived in what is now called Mexico City, disease, destruction and misery were rampant. They were able to make few converts to Catholicism under the repressive and brutal regime that was imposed by the Spaniards. All Aztec places of worship had

Mexico

been systematically destroyed. By 1531, when these apparitions of Mary occurred, the original Aztec citizens of Mexico City were depressed, beaten down, demoralized and humiliated. Most were practicing their native religion in secret. As word of the miraculous occurrence at Tepeyac spread, and people saw the *tilma* (robe) with the image of Our Lady of Guadalupe, the Franciscans were besieged with new converts. Within eight years, 10 million Mesoamericans living in Mexico City converted to Catholicism.

Though the image of Our Lady of Guadalupe had relevant meaning for the Europeans, the Aztec people felt that the image on the tilma was speaking to them in a very personal way. The Mesoamericans had a very complex, nonlinear writing style utilizing pictorial images. The coded image she brought to the Aztecs is very detailed and would take much study to understand. The womblike shape around the image, the rays of the sun, the crest of the moon, the folds of the robe, the subdued serpent, the colors worn by the Virgin—all had very direct messages to deliver to the Aztecs. It is thought that one of the announcements the Virgin is making is the birth of the age of the sixth sun. The Aztecs broke up their history into solar ages. The fifth sun, the sun of movement, was ended with the conquest. The new age was called the sun of flowers. It was considered an age for humanity to come into its own and bloom. The birth of a new sun always occurs after a time of great darkness, much like the sun rises after the night. To the Aztecs, the arrival of the Europeans represented the destruction of their culture, the appearance of the Virgin after ten years of darkness represented the dawn of this new age that was to be born through her appearance. The robe of the Virgin is touching the angel. To the Aztecs this symbolized a kiss. Since

EL GRANDE TEMPLO D MEXICO

the angel represents all of mankind, the main message of Mary is one of love, protection and affection.

To the Christians, the iconography of this image of Mary was very traditional. In Revelation, Saint John says: "A great sign appeared in the heavens, a woman clothed with the sun." This image is associated with the Immaculate Conception. In 1531, December 9 was the day recognized by both Eastern and Western Churches as the day the feast of the Holy Conception of Mary was celebrated. (In the Western Church it has since been moved to December 8.) This was also the first day that Mary appeared to Juan Diego. To each culture she imparts a different set of symbols, yet she enables both groups to come together in mutual agreement: The Virgin of Guadalupe is announcing a new age in humanity.

Perhaps the greatest miracle wrought by Our Lady of Guadalupe was the changes she brought to two violent cultures, the Spanish Europeans and the Aztecs. When the conquistadores arrived in Mexico City it is estimated that one in five chil-

Mexico

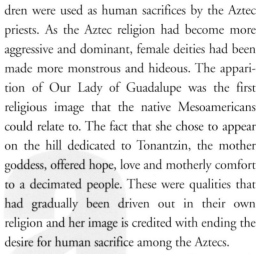

dren were used as human sacrifices by the Aztec priests. As the Aztec religion had become more aggressive and dominant, female deities had been made more monstrous and hideous. The apparition of Our Lady of Guadalupe was the first religious image that the native Mesoamericans could relate to. The fact that she chose to appear on the hill dedicated to Tonantzin, the mother goddess, offered hope, love and motherly comfort to a decimated people. These were qualities that had gradually been driven out in their own religion and her image is credited with ending the desire for human sacrifice among the Aztecs.

At the time of the apparitions, the Spaniards were looting Mexico City of its gold and treating the native population as subhuman. In Spain the Inquisition was occurring: Jews and Muslims were tortured into converting to Christianity or driven out of Spain altogether. This apparition of Mary softened the brutal fundamentalist approach to dogma and changed the way Catholicism was practiced in Mexico. The image on Juan Diego's tilma is a fusion of Byzantine and Aztec art. By embracing both cultures and declaring herself a source of motherly compassion for all of mankind, she forced both groups to gradually combine into a new mixed race of people, practicing their faith in a more loving way.

Tepeyac and the Basilica of Our Lady of Guadalupe are part of Mexico City. In 1976, a new Basilica of Our Lady of Guadalupe was built that holds the cloak of Juan Diego. It has the capacity to hold ten thousand people. The yearly pilgrimage is a major holiday in Mexico spanning December 9 to December 12. The image of Our Lady of Guadalupe is one that transcends organized religion: Her message of solace and motherly protection of all people makes her the most popular and loved incarnation of Mary.